Magnificent Addiction

Philip R. Kavanaugh, M.D.

Aslan Publishing
PO Box 108
Lower Lake, CA 95457

Published by

Aslan Publishing
P.O. Box 108
Lower Lake, CA 95457
(707) 995-1861

For a free catalog of our other titles,
or to order more copies of this book
please call (800) 275-2606

Library of Congress Cataloging-in-Publication Data:

Kavanaugh, Philip, 1931-
    Magnificent addiction : discovering addiction as gateway to
healing / Philip Kavanaugh. -- 1st ed.
          p. cm.
    ISBN 0-944031-36-6 : $12.95
    1. Compulsive behavior--Religious aspects. 2. Substance abuse-
-Religious aspects. 3. Control (Psychology)--Religious aspects.
4. Compulsive behavior--Patients--Religious life. I. Title.
RC533.K38 1992
616.85'227--dc20   91-41755
                                                                    CIP

Copyright © 1992, Philip Kavanaugh

Cover design by Brenda Plowman and Dawson Church
Cover artwork produced by Scott Lamorte

Printed in USA
First Edition

10 9 8 7 6 5 4 3 2

DEDICATION

This book is dedicated to many people in my life. Some of them, unfortunately, are no longer here to receive this tribute.

To Dad and Mother and your seven sons, the "seven fightin' Irish" as we were called. Particularly my three eldest brothers, Frank, John, and Bob. You died without knowing how well you served others, or how much you influenced what I believe and write.

Especially to you, Bob. You loved everyone so unselfishly and you are beside me often offering your presence and your strength.

Please continue to be there from time to time, when I forget, or when I listen to lies my ego tells me—like the ones I believed for so many years.

To my wife, Nancy, a gift from a Power beyond my conception. You offer me the comfort and support I am not able to provide myself. You are, indeed, a healer's healer.

To my children, Frank, Mary, Bob, Judy, Amy, and Liz. You were often my best teachers, and the source of my strength in transition. Your evolving lives are a continuing testimony to the power of your own healing process.

To Jamie, brother and lifelong friend. Your love and disciplined dedication were there during my darkest times, and as I watch your evolution I am more accepting of my own.

To the many people I have been privileged to know as my patients in more than thirty years as a physician and psychiatrist. Each of you has been my teacher and those lessons are included here.

To my friends and colleagues. Especially those of you who kept faith in me during the years I was much further from peace than I am now. You too have been and continue to be my teachers.

To Pat, Anita, Joy, Brenda, Arnie, Roger, Celeste, Penny, Diana, Molly, Frank, Bruce, Diane, Jane, Paula, and others of the staff at Los Gatos Therapy Center for their input and support. Especially to David Richer, who numerous times helped tame this dinosaur of a book and turn it into a readable being.

And, finally, to all those unnamed people who have helped and supported me as I progressed from being wounded to discover the keys to Healing.

I love all of you and offer you my version of *Magnificent Addiction.*

Table of Contents

INTRODUCTION

*What we concentrate on becomes our reality. If we
concentrate on fear we become ill and if we concentrate
on illness, we become crippled. On the other hand if we
concentrate on the limitless we can become that as well.*
—BARTHOLOMEW, REFLECTIONS OF AN ELDER BROTHER

Who would have predicted that after more than twenty years as
a psychiatrist I would experience an emotional breakdown and
become a patient? Not me. But I did. And who would have anticipat-
ed that even though my symptoms were mostly anxiety and depression, not alcoholism or drug dependence, I would discover that I was
an addict? Once more, not me. But I am. And who would have con-
ceived that addiction would not only prove to be the root of my
breakdown but the key to my healing as well, and that I would today
view addiction as the heart of a hopeful program of healing? Certainly not me. But it is.

These startling conclusions grew from a series of unwanted, and
certainly unplanned experiences which I lived through over a several
year period. I changed my thinking dramatically during those turbu-
lent times and made drastic changes in the way I practice as a psychiatrist. As an example, I discovered that addiction, which literally

means "to surrender or give over control," involves a lot more than destructive behaviors or an unholy attachment to booze and drugs.

I have learned to think of addiction as an energy that is intimately intertwined with healing and creativity, not just a destructive force that we must try to eliminate from our lives. The image I now hold of addiction is one of a powerful energy that can be expressed in countless ways, depending on our beliefs and our thoughts. In and of itself this addictive energy is neither positive nor negative. Like a fuel it can be used for creative or destructive purposes, depending on how we choose to employ it. It is through our thoughts and ideas that we make or fail to make these choices. That energy is working for us or against us.

Addictions such as alcohol and drugs are perversions of our creativity and involve misdirecting our addictive energy. Whenever our thoughts and beliefs are driven by fear, we generally experience much pain. We would do anything, it seems, to control this fear and pain. Most often we believe we can escape if we control the external world, manipulate other people or things to behave in ways that will allow us to feel secure. Or we may believe that the way to control the discomfort is to numb ourselves to it. Either set of thoughts and beliefs can direct us to the misuse of our addictive energy. We may attach our creative energy to a person, a group, a substance, or a pattern of behaving which at least temporarily relieves us of our fears and pain. But in doing this we stifle our creativity. We soon find ourselves frustrated, our fears increasing rather than decreasing. We are unable to find "full-fill-ment" because we are expending our addictive energy in ways that benefit no one, least of all ourselves.

It is possible to see how the patterns of unhealthy addictions are set up in our lives, not by the presence of the addictive energy, nor even through the presence of a so-called "addictive substance" or relationship, but by the thought or belief that we can successfully control our fear and pain in these ways. What's more, emotional breakdowns like the one I experienced, and disabling physical illnesses, begin the same way. Both begin in our thoughts and beliefs, as misperceptions about how to control and express our addictive energy.

As I detail in this book, there are many symptoms of addiction, but they all involve the same energy. What I have learned is that it is not the addictive energy itself that we must strive to eliminate or change. On the contrary, it is in this addictive energy that we find our salvation. To seek to control or subdue it, if that were really possible, would be to eliminate our creativity as well. The answer lies in choosing very carefully how we use this energy, making certain that what we become addicted to truly serves us and everyone around us.

I no longer try to help my patients understand or overcome their addictions. It is a futile, never-ending, and impossible task. I know why alcoholics evolve into chocolate junkies, or love addicts, or cling to their cigarette habit, and I know why people with emotional breakdowns relapse again and again. It is because they continue to focus their creative-addictive energies in unhealthy ways and persist in looking for manifestations of love in all the wrong places. But there is a better way, one that I was fortunate enough to discover in my own healing journey. It is the way I describe here.

In my practice I now encourage my patients to search in the places and ways that I know worked for me and have worked for thousands of others. I teach them how they can gently and gradually *"upgrade"* their addictions, how they can evolve to less destructive attachments and become less and less focused and dependent on alliances that will serve only to move them sideways in their lives rather than forward. In this way they are able to find more rewarding expressions for their addictive energy and begin to heal. They find full-fill-ment through more creative expression of their energy rather than degenerating and having their symptoms worsen.

It is no longer a mystery to me why genius and insanity are so often linked or why unhealthy addictions and emotional disorders are connected. They are all expressions of this universal addictive energy. We are all addicts in that we are constantly seeking to find more satisfying ways to move beyond mere survival and destructive directions and experience the deep full-fill-ment that comes with the creative expression of this energy. We are all born with the addictive energy and the drives that go with it. We all experience this energy's constant appeal for fulfillment. We vary as individuals only in how we express it, and whether or not our chosen expression "full-fills" and satisfies us or leads to emptiness and destruction.

All of the myriad ways that addictive energy is expressed in unhealthy or destructive ways are nothing more than symptoms of misguided thoughts and beliefs. Our beliefs generate our feelings and determine whether we feel fear and pain or peace and joy. This addictive energy is part of an inner force that we can use to support and strengthen our wellness and healing or plunge ourselves into breakdowns, emotional dysfunction, substance abuse, and destructive relationships. The addictive energy that is in all of us then fuels not only our destructive cravings, fears, and anxieties but our search for positive answers and the experience of our creative purpose as well.

What we often call addictions are the result of our seeking to control the expression of this energy in ways that only temporarily satisfy us or relieve our fears and pain. Eventually they all lead to disappointment. Most often what we are trying to control are our own unwanted or fearful feelings. Such efforts ultimately fail because fearful feelings reflect fearful thoughts and beliefs. These feelings are beyond our power to change until we change our ideas and beliefs. These failures result from misdirecting our addictive energy and can come about when we listen to our ego's self-centered ambitions and goals, goals which do not achieve our true purpose. We can begin to discover this purpose by learning to listen to a quiet inner voice instead, a voice which reflects our intuition and feelings, a softer voice that will lead us to our creative source as we simply "do nothing" and listen to its prompting.

No, indeed, it is not addictive energy itself but the actions, substances, or relationships that we choose for its expression that determine whether we ultimately heal or destroy ourselves.

What breaks down or collapses when our lives unravel is not our nerves or emotions, though these clearly are affected. Rather, what breaks down and ceases to support us is our self-perception, our thoughts, and our beliefs. Perhaps we can say more accurately that what breaks down are our mis-beliefs that we once believed were our salvation. The principles and faith that we learned to rely on to guide our lives and give us confidence turn out to be flawed; the sources of comfort we chose have failed us, because they provide us with only brief, sadly inadequate satisfaction or fleeting pleasure instead of the true peace and full-fill-ment that our addictive energy is prompting us to seek.

With a breakdown we come face to face with the fact that the fragmented images that our perceptions, thoughts, and beliefs have been providing us, fall far short of what we need to full-fill our creative purpose. Our unhealthy addictions develop as the result of following beliefs that simply cannot sustain us in our search for peace and contentment.It is those failures of our beliefs that cause our pain, not the addictive behaviors, people, or objects that we have desperately sought to offset the shortcomings of those beliefs.

Pain, no matter how we experience it, can dissolve all of our illusions and shatter our beliefs or our misbeliefs. It can prod us to pay close attention to what is happening inside us and guide us to an entirely new set of beliefs—one that is learned from paying attention to our own intuition and inner feelings. It is usually pain of some kind that prompts us to seek new beliefs which, in turn, allow us to express the creative source that is so much a part of us all. Through this process of experiencing pain and searching for more appropriate expressions of our addictive energy, we can begin to change our lives. We can discover new answers,—ones which will not only end our suffering but will also offer us peace, joy, and full-fill-ment. At such times in our lives, our breakdowns become our "break-throughs."

Addiction, I am convinced, can only be healed by another addiction. This usually rings true for anyone who has confronted addictive forces in him or herself or has lived with a person who lives in denial and refuses to face these forces. In order to heal unhealthy addictions or emotional breakdowns, a mighty force is needed. It must be one that is powerful enough to combat thoughts of suicide or the decision to trade a loving family or a promising career for booze, drugs, gambling, or sex. Only such a powerful force can effectively counteract the potent energy that unhealthy addictions generate. I learned this lesson again and again during my painful time. Medication can quiet the symptoms. Psychotherapy can help. But I learned there is more.

I discovered my own healing path, the one I describe in this book, quite by accident and mostly by accepting that my ways of living and believing had failed. I had to learn to have a willingness to listen to my friends and give over control of my beliefs and my life to others and to a power greater than myself. I learned that I had given my power to idols and beliefs which could not sustain me through my emotional breakdown and I was forced to look elsewhere for my answers. I'm grateful that I did because in the process I discovered that addiction to a system of spiritual beliefs can offer a potent enough force to overcome virtually any unhealthy symptoms; it can bring peace, joy, and love into a life once dominated by chaos, pain, and fear.

My search for the healing addiction and the journey that I took beyond the pain, fear, and chaos that I had created in my life provided me with the opportunity to create the healing program that is the subject of this book. It is through this program that I and many, many others have at last discovered that what we once believed to be our greatest weakness could become our greatest strength. The addictive energy we once feared and believed to be the source of our pain is here transformed.

Finally it is our MAGNIFICENT ADDICTION.

PART

1

The
Breakdown
Process

THE MAKING OF A PSYCHIATRIST

Each patient who comes to a therapist offers him a chance to heal himself. He is therefore his therapist. And every therapist must learn to heal from every patient who comes to him. He thus becomes his patient's patient.

—A COURSE IN MIRACLES,
PSYCHOTHERAPY, PURPOSE, PROCESS AND PRACTICE

Most people I have met during my thirty-plus years as a psychiatrist assume that people who specialize in healing other people's minds and emotions are somehow immune to breakdowns themselves or never succumb to unhealthy addictions, family tragedies, or life-threatening illnesses. I always notice how differently people relate to me when they discover that I am a psychiatrist. They assume that my training has not only given me mind-reading abilities and a burning desire to "analyze" them on the spot, but an absolute protection from personal problems, and the golden key to happiness and peace of mind as well. It hasn't, as my story will make clear. Psychiatrists have the same human strengths and weaknesses and face the same daily struggles as everyone else.

What we learn during our professional training, even with the added advantage of undergoing personal psychotherapy, does not give us any immunity from personal pain. And, at this point in my

15

life, I am grateful that it doesn't. Our humanness can offer our patients an added dimension of compassion and understanding which those who come for help often find reassuring. My vulnerability often comes as a pleasant surprise to my patients; it makes them more comfortable in relating to me, rather than prompting them to look elsewhere for help, as I might have feared.

More and more healers, like myself, are beginning to admit their humanness and are "coming out of the closet." Our openness is exactly the opposite of what we were taught to offer our patients; it kindles trust and confidence, which helps them heal, not fear and confusion, as we were taught to believe. Our wounds can heal like mine are healing, and our experience can offer hope and guidance far beyond the value of our skill in prescribing medication or therapy techniques that we learned from textbooks or from fellow therapists.

Certainly the knowledge I gained from the study of psychiatry and medicine is essential in my work. But patients can gain much more from the combination of my professional skill *and* the valuable lessons I learned by confronting and resolving the personal challenges and problems that I describe here.

The Beginning

Neither of my parents finished high school, yet both of them were fiercely resolved that their seven sons would have the education they lacked. And we did. Four of us became physicians—two obstetricians, a dentist, and a psychiatrist—two others became Catholic priests. Our education and success became the expression of our parents' thwarted ambitions. We felt that. Even as a young boy I knew I was going to become a priest, a doctor, or a member of another educated profession.

There was never any question.

The formal education of the seven sons of Hazel and Frank Kavanaugh (almost exclusively in Catholic institutions) totaled 143 years. Fortunately, the GI Bill helped pay for my two eldest brothers' college and graduate school, the Catholic church underwrote most costs for priesthood training, but dad and mother spent much of their limited income and meager savings on educating us and supporting their dream. Their dream became our lives.

One summer, years after I left home in Kalamazoo, Michigan, I visited my parents on vacation. Dad was seventy-four. He had recently retired from the insurance business after working continuously since graduating from eighth grade. He was straining under the weight of all those years of repressing his feelings and living mostly for others; he was not adjusting well to his new found leisure. He was feisty, outspoken, and less happy than I had ever seen him.

In all the years I knew him, he mostly worked, loved our mother, and took fierce pride in whatever activity any of his seven sons was involved. I can recall only a few brief vacations, several years of heavy drinking, and some trips to the hospital for various illnesses that marked the years prior to his retirement, which was forced by his declining health.

Sometime during that visit, dad declared mother was the source of his unhappiness. For the first time in my memory he criticized her. Growing up we were not allowed to raise our voices to mother without incurring his wrath. Now it was his turn. He followed her from room to room, listing her faults, citing his grievances, and declaring he was going to move to California, "where the real people live," referring to myself and two of my brothers, who had left the family fortress in Michigan to find freedom in the West. Possibly our bid for freedom triggered his.

Mother, realizing dad was "not himself," listened patiently and said nothing, which was unlike her. She was convinced that she had done the best she could.

The decision to travel to California seemed to me to be dad's long delayed, last ditch effort to express his pent-up frustration; it was a feeble rebellion against a life of conformity, duty, and living his dreams through his sons.

When he arrived in California, he quickly established the same routines he followed at home: morning coffee in an oversized cup, Camel cigarettes, and a three-hour trip through the morning newspaper, always ending with the crossword puzzle, which he solved seemingly with ease. Then he would sit at the table writing long letters to mother in his nearly illegible scrawl—the same scrawl that I remembered from his weekly letters to me while in college.

After three weeks, he obviously was missing her. He phoned her daily and their conversations grew lengthy and friendlier. Finally one night at dinner he tersely declared, "I'm going to give her another chance!" Mother had made reservations for him to return home and he was flying back to Michigan the following day.

My brothers and I drove him to the San Francisco airport. He rode in a wheelchair from the car—his legs had become so weak he could barely walk. But he sat up straight as we propelled him toward the departure gate. When the airlines attendant took over at the boarding gate and started to wheel him onto the plane, dad turned, looked back at three sons, and smiled. I have never forgotten that smile. It was the smile of a proud and satisfied man. A smile that clearly expressed his pride in each of us and his satisfaction in a life well lived, his job well done. He accepted that supporting us was reward enough. Satisfied with his life, he was returning home.

He died the next year from a ruptured aneurysm. He died quickly, without pain, and without any of us really saying goodbye. But that was typical of dad. He always hated goodbyes.

Mother, too, loved each of us, in the only way that she knew. She "did" for us. Her nearly limitless energy never diminished for more than ninety years. Her steadfast devotion to her Catholic beliefs never wavered during that time, nor did her conviction that those same beliefs were universal in their relevance.

Catholicism was the focus of mother's life. She was raised in Chicago by a stern German father, who owned a small bakery, and his Irish immigrant wife. The powerful influence of the nuns permanently penetrated her consciousness. The nuns recognized and encouraged her lively intelligence and her myriad interests. She could draw, paint, and print beautifully. She was a textbook of spelling and grammar and seemed to remember the Latin she had learned, verbatim. Her family's poverty had forced her to channel all of these gifts into typing and shorthand, except that somehow her mother had sequestered enough money for piano lessons and at family gatherings.mother would play any tune we could hum.

Her formal education ended at fifteen when she became a "steno-grapher" as she called it. She brought her weekly paycheck home to her mother, receiving back only enough to ride the streetcar with her lunch in a paper sack and buy a weekly treat. She married dad when she was twenty-three, just as she and her numerous Irish aunts were beginning to fear that she would be an oldmaid. The nuns had given mother the love her own too busy and overwhelmed parents could not, and mother's loyalty to all nuns reflected her gratitude.

People were measured by whether or not they were Catholic; friends, by whether or not their families were "good Catholics." The pastor's word was law in our home—above dad's. A fear of authori-ty transferred from mother's own stern and austere father was pro-jected into all men, dad, the Monsignor and her God. She extolled sacrifice. And her life reflected her message. She supported every aspect of the church: daily mass at 6:30, evening devotions, seven altar boy sons who learned their Latin responses under her careful supervision. She chauffeured the nuns, baked for parish events, and offered any priest or seminarian a home away from home. She prose-lytized converts, picking them up and delivering them to Catholic instruction classes. She often lamented that she had not entered the convent herself. There were times when we lamented it too.

Her fervor for Catholicism exacted a great expense in other areas of her life. Her intellectual curiosity was absent. I never saw her read a book that was not somehow connected with Catholicism. For a while she became fascinated with accounts of demonic possession, and we found magazines with explicit sexual accounts of young women possessed by devils hidden under her mattress. She was fru-gal with praise, incessantly critical, except when we could somehow distract her and make her laugh. She loved to laugh. Mother was exquisitely self-conscious, seemingly the result of a noticeable birth mark on her face. Others saw her as perky and cute. She saw herself as homely and had a habit of turning her face sideways when she was introduced to a new person.

She pushed us as much as she withdrew. Her favorite expression was "you have a Kavanaugh face," whatever that meant.

Because of her abbreviated education and her fears of people, she preached constantly for us to always stand up for what we believed.

This caused a few minor fights for us as kids, but created many more difficult problems for mother when her two priest sons left the priesthood and three other sons stopped attending the Catholic church.Whenever we spoke, her first question was always "Are you still in the church?"

Looking back from today, childhood seems happy. Yet for years, I carried painful wounds from the fierce, unrelenting control over my life exerted by a woman barely five feet two inches in height. I practiced what she was, not what she preached. Her control became my control, as did her fear of people. Her self-consciousness lived deeply inside me. Her critical nature became my nature. Her competitiveness became my constant companion. There was no escaping. I became a perfectionist, but only in areas important to my parents. Dad loved sports. I participated in five sports in our small Catholic high school. Mother loved academics and the church. There I excelled. At least, I excelled in school. As for church, I knew even in grade school that I was only going through the motions, but I was too afraid to challenge either mother or my own fears of going to hell.

One of my clearest childhood memories is of the"missionaries," priests who worked among the "pagans" in China and South America, seeking to make converts. They came to our parish yearly, usually asking for money from the adults, and telling us kids how one must "risk" for Christ if called upon. We must be ready to be martyrs like the early Christians in the event our faith was threatened by Communists or others hostile to Catholicism.

I knew that if called upon to be martyred for Christ, I would align myself with the pagans to stay alive. I was never that committed to Catholicism.

My harshest criticism, like most people, was reserved for myself. My parents' focus became my own. Mother's feelings of homeliness became my obsession with being skinny, or for having a "bullet-shaped," head after being called "bullet-head" by a fourth-grade classmate. I avoided situations where my "skinniness" might be exposed—beaches, swimming pools, and health clubs. Additionally I had inherited "Kavanaugh feet" with crooked toes, which added to my self-consciousness. This led to years of near obsessive gym visits.

And I endured four operations on my feet, each helping to disfigure them a bit more. I often remarked, "if I had spent as much time developing my body as I spent in church, I would be an Adonis." Hardly true, but it assuaged my self-consciousness for a while. Truly the sins (and the hang-ups) of parents pass through many generations of their offspring.

Fortunately, both my parents loved to laugh. I became expert (along with my brother Jamie) at entertaining them. I never complained about my entertainment skill during the years I berated them for their "abuse," religious and otherwise.

I blamed my parents for the unhappiness I felt until I learned through my own breakdown and healing the wonderful healing power of forgiveness.

Continuing the Journey

For many years I wondered why I became a psychiatrist. I cannot even count how many times I have been asked that question in my years in the field.

Our home in Kalamazoo, Michigan, was just two blocks from a large state mental hospital made up of numerous redbrick buildings with barred windows and large porches covered with heavy wire. There the patients sat and looked out. The spacious hospital grounds became our playground and the patients our spectators, and sometimes friends. Patients lived for months or years during those pretranquilizer years, waiting for their demons to quiet. Many recovered in time and left. Others were there throughout my childhood, and I presume they died there.

To me the patients were interesting people and I felt a keen interest in them even as a child talking with them and asking for their views. I was immensely curious about how these people were different than me. Maybe that spurred my interest in psychotherapy. During high school, two older brothers Bob and Jamie, left for the seminary, headed for the priesthood. This delighted mother. I have often remarked that the priesthood is the noblest way for a Catholic mother to never have to relinquish her son(s) to another woman. I believe it is true. I recall my dad lamenting that both of them would have

been great insurance salesmen. I think he envisioned we might all
one day join him in business and have an insurance dynasty, a peas-
ant version of the Kennedys.

Later, my brothers left the priesthood and joined me in California. Dad never seemed disappointed, and even mother could understand their leaving, since she was aware of the politics in the Church
and she felt both brothers had been undervalued. However, she
could not abide their marrying, which both did shortly after leaving
the priesthood.

Having two priest sons seemed to lessen mother's interest in my
choosing that holy profession. She joked that I would become a
"garbage man for the Jesuits," after I entered the pre-med program at
Marquette University (run by the Jesuits), implying that eventually I
would follow the lead of my brothers. But, clearly, the heat was off,
and mother was quite satisfied (as was dad) when I began pre-med
classes.

I know there is a connection for me, between psychiatry and the
priesthood. Even when I was in pre-med I knew I would become a
psychiatrist. I never seriously considered any other specialty. I was
not attracted to science, satisfied only the necessary science requirements for admission to medical school and selected elective courses
in philosophy whenever I could.

Medical school and Internship were a means to an end. I disliked
the rigorous pace, but I was used to sacrifice and hard work and
found it a challenge. I always did best in classes that involved taking
care of patients. I was less good in purely scientific endeavors. I continued to lean toward psychiatry, so much so that I avoided psychiatric classes, and stressed other areas, because I knew I was headed
for psychiatry.

My friends and strangers would always ask, "Why do you want
to be a psychiatrist?" My answer then was that I didn't want to be a
priest because I wanted to be married; I was not good enough with
my hands to be a surgeon; and I was attracted to the idea of treating
the "whole person." From my vantage point today, however, I recognize that I was attracted to psychiatry for more than these reasons.
The lure was there because of a restless, impatient energy that compelled me towards learning about and healing myself through my

interaction with patients. I am not putting myself down by that admission, since I believe most people choose their professions, their spouses, even their life-styles for similar, unconscious reasons associated with unresolved parts of their lives. No one is unique in that respect.

That energy remains today, though I am no longer restless and impatient. It has been softened by experience, humbled and tempered by my breakdown, and as I heal, it often glows within, like a joyful beacon discovered after years of searching, suffering, and finally surrendering.

I believe that when we misdirect that energy, it expresses itself in unhealthy addictions and emotional disorders. When we follow its guidance to its source within, I believe it is experienced differently, as peace of mind and serenity. This same energy redirected becomes the energy of Spirit—our magnificent addiction.

Becoming a Psychiatrist

I began psychiatric training at Johns Hopkins Medical Center in Baltimore in 1957. I was twenty-five and had just completed my internship at Receiving Hospital in Detroit. My 1952 Ford coupe, my books, and my few belongings were my only companions on the 600-mile journey between the two hospitals. I had never been that scared. Although I had been away from home for college and medical school, this was my introduction to a world away from the familiar sub-culture of my large family and the trappings of Catholicism.

Fortunately for me, when I arrived at Johns Hopkins, the psychiatric staff reflected the maturity of the stately, old buildings. Psychiatric patients were housed in an ancient four-story, ivy-covered, brick building named the Henry Phipps Psychiatric Clinic (shortened to HPPC) after a generous donor. Johns Hopkins (named for a prosperous merchant and rum runner who donated funds for the hospital) was a mature institution and the attitude toward training young doctors was similar to a wise grandparent. This contrasted to the anxious-parent atmosphere I had been accustomed to in the Midwest. The atmosphere in the hospital was scholarly and accepting. Instead of teaching us rigid rules about caring for patients and interpreting their behaviors, which many psychiatric centers were doing in those years, we were encouraged to relate to patients using our own style and develop our own techniques.

"Patients really want to get well," my first clinical instructor, John Hansen, told me. "There is something inherent in the body that seeks to be healed. Maybe the best advice I can give you is to be caring, stay out of their way, and they will recover if they are going to recover."

This experience was so unlike my years growing up in a Catholic family and my education in Catholic schools, where everything was more certain, structured, and controlled. At times during the years of psychiatric training, I protested there was not enough "structure." I had become dependent on direction and certainty in the Catholic system of education; this new freedom was unfamiliar and uncomfortable at first. However, I learned quickly to appreciate the liberating atmosphere at Johns Hopkins. This began my separation from Catholicism and made me reluctant to trust equally dogmatic theories in psychiatry reflected by the teachings of Sigmund Freud and his followers.

Psychoanalysis, as that theory is called, was the most popular model of psychiatry in the 1950s. As I became more liberated from the dogmatism (defined as reason devoid of emotions) of my Catholic background, I was immediately suspect of the complicated and equally dogmatic teachings of psychoanalysis. Even though psychoanalysts opposed orthodox religious ideas like those I had been taught in Catholicism, they were as dogmatic in their own pronouncements. When any of us asked questions, we were told, "you won't understand this until you have had you own analysis." It was reminiscent of the "mysteries" in Catholic theology that I had already begun to question.

Even more frustrating for me, the answers psychoanalysts offered lacked practical application to patients and clinical problems. I recall a particular patient I was treating during my first year of psychiatric training, whose problems were deeply troubling me.

Sylvia was severely depressed. She had been transferred to the Johns Hopkins psychiatric unit after she tried to kill herself by overdosing with sleeping pills. She was then a 36-year-old mother of six children, all under twelve years old. Her emotional circuits were so overloaded that this breakdown and trip to the psychiatric unit was her only vacation in the thirteen years since her honeymoon.

She was a petite, haggard-looking woman, barely five feet tall, with fine, stringy red hair that was uncombed. I often wondered how this tiny woman could have carried and borne six children. She seldom looked at me during our early meetings. She felt very guilty and ashamed of having tried to kill herself and could offer no explanation that lessened her guilt. At the same time she expressed disappointment that she had failed. This was further evidence of her inability "to do anythin' right." She was a desperate and unhappy woman. I was a frustrated first-year psychiatric resident, long on compassion but very short on answers for this tiny, sad woman.

Her husband, Gene, was in striking contrast to Sylvia. He was poised, polished, always well-groomed and seemed oblivious to Sylvia's problems. He would call every few days, but only ask me, "Is she ready to come home yet?" I felt anger towards him, I recall. I offered him little in the way of answers or support. Today, I understand how desperate and afraid he must have been too.

I discussed my concerns at a staff conference of psychoanalysts. I tried to apply their answers since I had none of my own.I followed the psychoanalysts suggestions, though I felt awkward. I plunged into asking her about anger towards her father which she had most likely "repressed," but which my instructors insisted was the underlying cause of her depression. Forget her circumstances. Ignore her overwhelming responsibilities, lack of support, and low self-esteem. Hit her with her unconscious hostility. It simply didn't fit. Confronting her with this only added to her already deflated self-image. Not only was she guilty and a failure, but here were new reasons to feel guilty and ashamed. I was so desperate and frustrated. I knew, then, as I faced this tiny woman devoid of hope, that there had to be a better, more practical answer than I (and the "experts") offered her.

Questions I was already asking about Catholicism made me skeptical of any system that explained everything based on myths, essentially without proof. More important for me, though, in the case of Sylvia, was the fact that the methods did not produce results.

We were encouraged to trust our instincts and develop our own style by other psychiatrists on the Johns Hopkins staff who were not psychoanalysts. I composed twelve *Lessons In Living*, based on a common-sense approach. With the help of a maverick professor, Jerome Frank, who supported and even encouraged my doubts about psychoanalysis, I began a therapy group based on those lessons. I realize now that those lessons appealed to me because they were quite structured, like Catholicism. I also realize those lessons were an early and very primitive model of the belief-changing program I followed during my healing and which I continue to practice and teach.

The central theme of the twelve lessons I composed with Dr. Frank's encouragement was that emotional disorders are not problems—they are answers. They are wrong answers. The task became one of finding, adopting, and reinforcing right answers. The lessons contained catchy slogans such as "erase and replace," "rehearse and reverse," and others equally poetic. Somewhere in my travels I lost those lessons, but I recall one titled "Right Answers, Can We Bear Them?" which stressed how we tend to resume old, familiar behaviors because we are "addicted" to our ways and they are very difficult to change. The use of a structured approach and the slogans were suggested to me by a self-help group named *Recovery Inc.*, established by Dr. Abraham Low, a Chicago psychiatrist, in the 1930s. I had learned about this organization while in medical school. One of my classmates had an emotional breakdown, dropped out of school for a year, and found this organization enormously helpful. The structured meetings, which use Dr. Low's book titled *Mental Health Through Will Training*, are helping thousands of patients today. The structure of the meetings, and the slogans in the textbook are similar to those used in 12-Step programs which I learned years later.

Patients in that first group experienced considerable improvement. Many of them nearly memorized the lessons, repeated the slogans over and over, and felt and functioned better. The slogans and the structure of the group gave them a common language to share, group support, and a united approach to their diverse problems. They loved it. So did I.

It was the first of many times as a psychiatrist that I asked myself, "Is this the answer?"

The other psychiatrists, it seemed to me, viewed my approach as too "simplistic," not sophisticated enough. I was exquisitely sensitive to their opinions and I soon abandoned this wonderfully simple approach. Not yet secure enough to follow my parents' repeated directive and stand up for myself, I changed to what the other psychiatrists in my group were learning to do: probe deeply into the human psyche, look for answers in each patient's history, make correct diagnoses, and attempt what I now call "data cures."

It would take me nearly ten years before I began to trust my intuition and feelings enough to initiate an independent course in treating patients. Only slowly did I develop a therapy style suited to me and based on what I observed and believed from my own experience.

I left Johns Hopkins after three years to become a Navy psychiatrist. The U.S. Government transported me and my young family from Baltimore to southern California, where I spent two years as a reserve officer and psychiatrist stationed at the San Diego Naval Hospital. An instructor of mine from Johns Hopkins had accepted a position nearby as Psychiatric Director of the Scripps Clinic and Research Foundation in La Jolla, a suburb of San Diego. He offered me an opportunity to "moonlight" at the clinic during my active Navy duty and I accepted. A year after leaving the Navy I opened my first private practice in La Jolla. The year was 1963.

Encounter Group Therapy— Getting in Touch with Feelings

The beginning of my most dramatic transformation began one Thursday in La Jolla. It was 1967. I had been practicing for several years and, in addition to my private practice, I had organized a small clinic focused on marital and family problems. A group of us therapists had organized a weekly lunch-time group, where we shared experiences, supported each other, and explored new ideas and approaches.

At this meeting, we heard a tape of an "encounter group," a new therapy method which stressed involving the participant's emotions (thus "encounter" was coined). This approach was being popularized at Esalen Institute at Big Sur, in northern California. We were instructed to stand in a tight circle with our arms around each other and stare continuously into each other's eyes. The tape, playing in the background, instructed us to become closer and more emotionally connected to one another. I found myself starting to sweat; my heart began speeding up, and I felt a huge lump in my chest. Then I panicked. I lost it.

After years of experience, the cool, competent, well-trained psychiatrist, was panicking when he began getting really close to other human beings. I was afraid to expose my "weakness," (and I was not certain what that meant) but I was more afraid of running than staying. I felt awful. I felt afraid, weak, shaky, and embarrassed. I dripped with perspiration.

That was my first "breakthrough" into my inner self. I had undergone some therapy and gained some insight and understanding of my family, background, etc. But this was different than any other therapy method I had experienced or read about. Very different. I was impressed and very interested.

My associates and I began using this approach almost immediately, conducting weekend encounter groups at a center nearby. Being the first psychiatrist in the area to use this new, "untried" method was controversial. We were controversial. We helped many of our patients. We helped them discover their emotions, often buried since childhood. And we made some mistakes. When someone suddenly connects with emotion (after years of suppression) they are apt to act impulsively, without reflection. And this happened. Encounter groups made it easier to express all feelings, both positive and negative ones. I now realize how difficult it was being a teacher and student simultaneously. But these groups marked the beginning of profound changes in our approach to people's emotions. There was nothing else available except cold, analytical psychiatry (I continue to recall Sylvia, my patient at Johns Hopkins).

An aura of excitement surrounded encounter groups because of all the possibilities they opened. Psychiatry has always talked about feelings. Here was a direct approach to feelings. In those years, everyone, therapists and their patients were searching, trying to find answers. The search was both exciting and painful, liberating and confusing, helpful and frightening. Yet the risks seemed worth the effort. We had no road map. We were guided only by the conviction that conventional ways of living and helping were inadequate.

On weekends, our staff and thirty of our patients met in small groups at a retreat setting near La Jolla. We set up exercises to encounter emotions and help each person move inside their emotional walls. An example would be to ask each person to go around the group and tell one thing they liked about each other person. Does it sound easy? It isn't, yet this simple exercise and similar ones helped many participants begin to experience submerged feelings, emotions buried beneath a sea of self-consciousness and fearful control. Patients experienced rage, love, laughter, sadness, joy, excitement—a range of feelings unfamiliar to most of them. There was marvelous energy in these groups. It was a spiritual experience, though we never called it that.

Again, when I saw dramatic changes in my structured groups, I asked myself the question, "Is this the answer?"

During those years, my psychiatric colleagues were often amused by my ever-changing approaches to therapy. I was always up on my latest discovery; always selling whatever technique I had come upon that benefitted my patients and myself. We held 24-hour marathon groups, weekend groups, non-stop groups, and five-day marathons. We allied with Fritz Perls and a group of therapeutic pioneers from Esalen Institute in Big Sur and other so-called growth centers in this feel to heal crusade.

The energy from these group experiences gradually faded. The high from these groups, I began to realize, resembled a drug-fix. It was a "people fix." The energy and excitement was not generated from inside. It came from the other members of the group. The course these groups followed was the same as unhealthy addictions, only the attachment was to people instead of drugs. And just as in drug addictions, the participants developed tolerance (each "fix" produced less of a high) to these experiences. Each group produced less excitement, less of a "high," and the effects lasted a shorter time. There was no way to preserve the effects, or take the energy home because it was infused by the other members and was not generated from within ourselves.

After nearly two years, I slowly realized that encounter groups were not "the answer" either. The glow always faded, and though patients spoke of them with enthusiasm their lives seldom changed very much. The groups marked a beginning of change, though, and a refreshing alternative to the limited options we had to offer psychiatric patients and each other before their arrival.

A problem remained. How could one develop the self-confidence and freedom experienced in encounter groups—on a continuing basis? How could we experience our feelings, not hurt others, and continue to love ourselves? Was there some way we could love ourselves as much as other members of those groups appeared to love us, and still maintain the confidence and freedom we felt in those groups? The solution seemed to be discovering a method to generate those same loving feelings within ourselves. But how?

Primal Scream Therapy—
Allowing Feelings to Be Felt

A new book published about that time seemed to provide the answer to this question. It became the next guidepost in my search for happiness, contentment, peace of mind, and serenity. The book, *The Primal Scream*, by Arthur Janov, a Beverly Hills psychologist, described a method that taught patients to "feel feelings and not act on them." Janov dramatically described a young patient who contacted his deepest feelings and "uttered a deep, penetrating, painful scream." The patient, presumably, was re-living his frightening journey from the womb into the world. The scream, his primal scream, became the title for the book, and the focus of an entire therapy movement.

Janov wrote, "feelings are intended to be felt, not analyzed, not understood, not talked about, but felt." For me, having recognized the limits of encounter groups, this made sense. People were encouraged to experience their feelings, sit with them, and not take action (as was the practice in most encounter groups).

"Feel feelings. Don't act on them" was the theme of this approach.

This new method stressing "feel what you feel" contrasted to the "do what you feel" of the encounter groups. Patients were encouraged to feel or sit with anger or other emotions until the energy of the emotion passed. Then they could decide whether or not to act on their feelings. Feelings plus immediate action equates with impulsiveness, while feelings plus time equates with rationality.

Almost immediately, I began encouraging my patients to experience their emotions, to "feel the feelings," alone, without the support of a group, and mostly without my being there. I named this method, Process. The instructions were simple: "lie motionless and experience whatever sensations, emotions, or feelings occur, without judging the feelings as right or wrong, good or bad. And remain with those feelings until they change or disappear." "All feelings are temporary," I reminded them. "Even happy ones." "Feelings have no morality," I told them. "They are neutral. The only purpose of a feeling is to be felt. Not analyzed, not understood, not explained, not rationalized, but felt." I still believe all these statements.

From that time twenty years ago, "feel your feelings—don't act on them" became one of my therapeutic trademarks. It remains a mainstay of my healing program. (And it drove my wife and kids to distraction during those years when I constantly uttered "feel your feelings" in every family crisis except when I was in crisis.)

This "feel-to-heal" movement provided me with some of the most humorous memories of my career.

One patient, hearing that I was offering Primal therapy (which in fact was not what I offered), was lying on the carpet in my waiting room, before our initial meeting—screaming. Others could hardly wait to get into my office to begin their "primals." Many, who read the book, mimicked what they read, and criticized me as a "fraud" when I suggested an alternative to their interpretation of "primals." They accused me of not "going by the book." It was a wild time.

It was better than many movies. I coined an expression "moving decisively sideways through life," when I noticed many of the same people from encounter groups now "having primals." It was old-time religion with a new twist. I saw dramatic results, though, and it was reassuring to think "this is it! I have finally found the way." Easy to conclude because change in the psychiatric infantry where I practice is painfully slow. We all need our dreams to sustain us. Like all dreams this one—that Primal Therapy offered "the answer"—faded too.

There was more to follow. Janov's insight left a legacy of a useful tool in helping me and my patients unravel the mystery of our lives. I have incorporated his "feel your feelings and don't act on them" into the Reparenting section of my program.

I benefitted from Janov's insight, as did my patients. This approach offers a valuable piece to the puzzle of life for me. I saw patients, alone, away from the contagious atmosphere of encounter groups getting in touch with their deepest feelings.

Once more, I asked that question "Is this the answer?" Once more it was not.

It took more than the accumulation of all my experiences through childhood and adolescence, pre-med years, medical school, psychiatric training, and the many years of searching as a psychiatrist to finally help me discover what I believe is "the answer."

Eventually it took the experiences following my emotional breakdown and afterward, the discovery of my addictiveness, its source in my beliefs, and the ultimate connection with my spirituality to teach me what is really involved in full healing. There I found answers that lie beyond traditional psychotherapy, beyond encounter groups and primal therapy, beyond any other treatment modality available to the psychiatrist.

I looked everywhere outside myself. Finally I looked inside where my pain forced me to look. The connections I discovered between my emotional illness, my addiction, and my spirituality opened a new world of possibilities and forms.

I finally found that the answer was not a single method or approach so much as a combination of approaches, pieces of a puzzle all blending together in an integrated way. I recognized that I was making the same mistake over and over because I believed there was a single piece to the puzzle, a magic bullet, a mental penicillin shot that would heal all the pain and bring peace of mind. Each of the discoveries that I mention was an important one. So were the lessons I learned in my residency. Yet each of them was only another missing piece.

The final piece for me would come in the form of a personal spirituality, quite different from what I learned to call spiritual during my earlier life. It came in the form of an addiction, one I learned to call the addiction that heals.

THE WOUNDED HEALER

So many positive changes in life begin with personal hardship — or an apparent tragedy. The events which transformed my life originated with such an event. What began as my greatest misfortune later emerged as my best and most convincing teacher.

On November 1, 1981, my world fell apart. I had a major emotional breakdown. At the time, my life and career appeared solidly intact. I was well established in psychiatric practice in Los Gatos, a suburban community in northern California, near San Jose. My wife and I had purchased a small house near Good Samaritan Hospital, where I was a staff psychiatrist. We intended to remodel it for my practice. After struggling for more than a year with the local bureaucracy, we succeeded in having the house rezoned for a small clinic. Plans were drawn up, and major remodeling was underway. As it neared completion, I was looking forward to a Christmas Open House in the new offices, which I would share with six other practitioners. After nearly twenty years of practicing psychiatry in virtual isolation the prospect of a group stirred happy memories of my own childhood, growing up in a family of seven brothers.

The mail arrived that morning around 10 o'clock. I stood by my office manager's desk, glancing at the envelopes, quickly tossing all the junk mail into a waste basket. I tore open any envelopes which looked like checks from insurance companies, and left the other mail stacked on the desk.

Then I saw it. I could feel my heart starting to race. My throat suddenly felt dry and my hands began to shake. It was a window envelope, from our bank, with a pink notice showing through the window. That was always bad news. A bounced check, an incorrect deposit, or worse, an overdrawn account. I ripped open the envelope, already anticipating the worst. Our budget had been exceeded, our lending limits exhausted by the "extras" we had added to the building. Each upgrade we chose added thousands, it seemed, to the bill. Our lender (recall it was a recession time and we were paying over 22 percent interest on our loans) had said no to our latest request for more money.

The news was much worse than I was prepared to handle. The notice said we were several thousand dollars overdrawn in our account. Our savings, always meager in raising six children, had long been exhausted, and my pride and shame prevented me from asking friends or relatives for further help. This was my dream and I was determined "to do it myself."

I was working longer hours in my practice than ever before. My earning capacity was at its limit. That single pink notice triggered a reaction in me I had never before experienced.

Suddenly I felt like a huge inner tube with the air escaping. As I deflated, I began to feel small, weak, alone, and helpless. I saw no options open to me. I panicked and began to cry. It was more than three and a half years before I recovered fully from that experience.

There were other stresses in my life during that same time. I had lived helplessly through the deaths of three of my six brothers from cancer, all during the last four years. Each of them was in their early fifties, and each was stricken without apparent warnings. I was especially close to Bob, a former Catholic priest who had always been a phone call away when I needed some "big brother" advice. His death earlier that year had seemed to take a part of me with him. Each of my brother's deaths seemed so inexplicable and terribly premature. I became obsessed with my health and every twinge or spasm in my body set my mind reeling through lists of symptoms of cancer I had learned in medical school. Feelings, especially fear, which I had always been able to control, began to control me. My sleep was disrupted. I dove into activities that had comforted me in the past without finding consolation. I enjoyed playing tennis, so I played frantically but without enjoyment. I found comfort in my work and tried to work constantly, but did not have much energy and I fatigued easily.

Sometime during the first year of my depression my marriage ended. Linda and I had married hastily ten years earlier, after lengthy and gut-wrenching divorces. Even before the depression began, we had grown in opposite directions and had discussed separation. Linda was younger and felt she had missed important experiences in becoming her own person (called Individuation these days). She did not want to be tied to a relationship. Her career was flourishing, the children were able to look after themselves, and she no longer wanted to be married to anyone. My depression only hastened the time when she left. It is painful for anyone to live around someone who is depressed, especially a loved one. The sense of helplessness and despair that depression conveys makes it more than an illness. It becomes a way of life. Anyone who has lived with or around emotional illness understands this. When Linda left, I was too depressed to feel strongly affected. For me, the pain of depression was much deeper than the anguish of separation and divorce.

My lack of energy from the depression gradually forced me to give up working at the hospital. I also reduced the number of patients I saw in my office because I was no longer able to concentrate well enough to function for more than a few hours each day. I slipped further and further. Some days the energy for taking a shower and getting dressed was more than I could manage. I would lie at home, in bed, hour after endless hour, waiting for the pain to subside. Nothing I tried seemed to relieve it. Sometimes it let up gradually as the day passed, and often in the evenings I felt almost normal. But each morning anxiety crept into my chest moments after I awoke. When I first woke up I was calm for just a few seconds; then that feeling returned. A few moments after that, the heaviness of depression returned too, and the daily pattern repeated itself.

My dear secretary, Ann, covered my absences at work when I called her to report another day (or week) of being unable to drag myself to work. The struggle continued, month after endless month. I never knew when I would be too stricken, anxious, depressed, or both, to get out of bed, let alone see patients.

I watched other people in their cars when I was driving. I noticed their laughter and saw them conversing amiably. I wondered how could they be happy or find anything to enjoy when my life was so joyless and empty. Nothing interested me. Everything I looked at seemed like cardboard and appeared in one color, gray. Years later, even after I recovered, I could still feel painful twinges when I drove past certain places on my route to the hospital, recalling those joyless feelings. I smile now when I recall that then I felt even too depressed to kill myself.

I have never known pain that compares with depression and its accompanying anxiety. It's pain unlike a headache, toothache, or any other physical pain. Pain everywhere. Pain so unfamiliar yet so constant, it was difficult to define. It was different from physical pain because I often despaired that it would ever end. Endless hours of hopeless emptiness and sadness. A complete absence of pleasure or joy, which made life seem futile and meaningless. A feeling of "forever and ever," like I had been taught to think of Hell. Pain, barely affected by exercise (when I was able to do it), amino acids, vitamins, health foods, or other changes in diet, massage or anything else I could manage to think of or do. It was far too deep to be reached by any of these.

Medication helped. At first, though I tried to treat myself, I clearly had a "fool" for a physician—myself. Accountants often mess up their check books, and attorneys seldom have Wills, but these are nothing compared to a psychiatrist who tries to treat his own breakdown. Now I understand that, but for more than a year I self-medicated (from samples in my office) with antidepressants and antianxiety medication. I felt ashamed of my "weakness" and found only temporary relief of my pain. Finally, my symptoms overcame my pride and shame and I sought outside help from another psychiatrist who was an expert in psychopharmacology. I only needed to visit him once. He advised me to double the dose of the antidepressant and increase the antianxiety medication until I was able to sleep through the night. Two weeks later on a Saturday morning I awoke free of depression for the first time in over a year. I could hardly believe the difference.

It was not until that moment that I believed that antidepressants actually relieve depression. Previously, I thought they simply disguised or masked symptoms, similar to alcohol. I used them for years with my patients, yet never truly believed in them. That Saturday my own relief melted all my resistance to admitting that medication could be life-saving; it was not simply a "crutch" for weak people, as I had so arrogantly believed.

Medication relieved the symptoms and it restored my hope that I could recover; I still did not feel joy or happiness. I felt a constant gnawing unhappiness. I often asked myself as I drove from home to my office, "Is this all there is?" Finally, after my efforts to reduce the number of patients failed to bring peace, I turned over my practice to another psychiatrist, rented my home, and moved to southern California. I stayed with my brother Jamie, where I devoted full time to recovering. By then I had improved enough to discontinue all antidepressant medication, but I was still taking benzodiazepines (the drugs most attacked by the media) for my anxiety. They continued to help significantly for several more months until I was able to stop taking all medication.

A few weeks after arriving in southern California, and not working for the first time since childhood, I noted a growing restlessness. I was still weak and exhausted, but I couldn't be still. I tried exercise, meditation, short trips—everything I could think of. They all helped for a moment, but the restlessness always returned quickly. I felt vaguely alone, as if there was an emptiness inside I wanted someone or something to fill but didn't know who or what that might be.

My restlessness grew daily. I became more and more impatient and felt I must have a solution. I began to feel "out of control." I needed to end this new pain. In just a few weeks I became deeply immersed in a relationship with a much younger woman. I burned up the telephone lines, the freeway, and the airlines in a frantic effort to find comfort and peace through that relationship. I was obsessed, frantic because the relationship could not satisfy what I was feeling, except briefly. Then the gnawing, insistent restlessness would begin again. Gradually I began to realize that I was involved in an "addictive" relationship. I was addicted.

Fortunately for me, a good friend, recognized the "addictive" quality of that relationship. He knew that there was alcoholism in my family background and suggested that I attend a 12-Step recovery group to find help with my addiction.

More fortunately, I followed his suggestion. I was able to end the addictive relationship but it left a gaping void in my life. I filled that emptiness by attending daily meetings of Al-Anon one of the 12-Step fellowships. For a while I became "addicted" to those groups. It was not a perfect solution, but an addiction to 12-Step meetings and the other members was a vast improvement for me. For the first time in months I was free of the crippling insecurity and pain of my unhealthy addiction.

I had heard of 12-Step programs for years. My dad had been a member of Alcoholics Anonymous while I was growing up, but I never thought of myself as an addict, let alone a candidate for a 12-Step group. I believed such programs were for "real addicts"—alcoholics, drug abusers, overeaters, or compulsive gamblers. I learned quickly how wrong I was.

Recovery from Emotional Addiction

It took my breakdown, lengthy recovery, and the discovery that I was an addict to teach me lessons I would have scoffed at earlier. The connection between my emotional breakdown and the addictive relationship made it impossible to deny my addictiveness. The incompleteness of what I learned and practiced as a psychiatrist was also clear to me. Complete recovery involves far more than I had ever considered. Much more than removing symptoms of anxiety and depression with adequate medication is necessary. How much deeper than in psychotherapy, encounter groups, primal therapy, or any other form of therapy were my answers found. I discovered that finding and applying a spiritual program had far more power to transform my life than did psychiatric methods, and it made it possible for me to experience happiness, contentment, peace, and joy for long periods of time. My new view of emotional breakdowns like mine as manifestations of addictions opened a new world of possibilities. Finding a spiritual solution made them a reality for me.

Psychiatric treatment has never been effective in treating addictions. Mine was no exception. When I was feeling out of control, I was not interested in the reasons. Psychotherapy only offered me a few hours of relief. Like all addicts I was only interested in getting my "fix." During my depression the medications—once I took the appropriate amounts—relieved the symptoms. Later the drug of choice was that addictive relationship. Depression and anxiety were merely other symptoms of my addiction. When I was no longer depressed and anxious, I transferred the energy which had fueled my emotional breakdown to an addictive relationship. All addictions I could see were symptoms of this restless energy which I now call "addictive energy."

This energy was the same one that had been surging in me since childhood. I can still recall a restless, unhappy feeling when I sat impatiently with my family at Church, or bored at home. That same feeling was clearly present throughout college, medical school, internship, psychiatric training, and practice. That energy quieted temporarily by activity, but it was the same force that fueled my anxiety and depression during my emotional breakdown. And it was the source of my enormous passion during the addictive relationship. In recovery that energy changed again and often became peace and joy. I found, or perhaps more accurately rediscovered, that there was a connection between that energy and my spirituality. But there were mighty hurdles that stalled my progress.

Control—The Master Addiction

A major insight occurred for me one night during an Alanon meeting when I was particularly restless and impatient. There was a husky young man in his twenties known as "Trucker." He usually came to the meetings directly from work and wore a grease-stained T-shirt, torn Levi's, a baseball cap, and several days' growth of beard. That night he began to talk. At first I was tremendously put off by his raspy voice—the result of too many cigarettes and too much booze. He described his major problem as a need to control his wife and small son. This constant need to tell them every move to make was destroying his marriage and affecting the little boy. He spoke of using the slogan "Let go and let God" which the 12-Step programs suggest for situations beyond our control. He described how he was trying unsuccessfully to give up having to control his wife rather than continue to try to dominate her and others in his life. I felt angry toward him at first and thought "what a macho jerk!" Yet as he continued talking I had a sense that my reaction was way out of proportion. I turned my judgment from him to me, and asked myself, "Why am I so bothered? Is Trucker mirroring something in me?"

Almost immediately I had my answer. Quite suddenly I forgot about his rough, macho exterior and his raspy voice. He was me. He began to cry. And I let go and started crying with him. I could see that the pattern of his life was indeed like my own. He was addicted to controlling other people in his life. I suddenly saw and accepted that I had the same addictive need—the need to be in control. We were not addicted to booze or drugs. I was not simply addicted to my work or to some other relationship. Trucker and I were both addicted to control. And I understood in that same moment the main expression of my addictive energy.

No other addiction can trigger such alarming withdrawal symptoms as when we lose or feel out of control. Suddenly I felt as if someone had ripped the blinders from my eyes. I could see my life with new clarity. In those few moments I realized that since earliest childhood, throughout my years in medical school, psychiatric training and practice, all my education and relationships were attempts to somehow feel in control of my life. My depression and anxiety were the painful results of feeling out of control or, worse yet, of always feeling that way. The addictive relationship which eventually drove me to seek out 12-Step meetings was another attempt to regain the control I had lost during my breakdown and when I gave up my psychiatric practice. In this flash of recognition, I was able to see that even joining Al-Anon was another attempt to find out how I could regain control in that relationship, not give it up as an unhealthy addiction.

Finally I realized I had found an answer I had sought for so many years. This was the correct diagnosis we were so thoroughly taught to seek as physicians. Now proper treatment could begin.

Growing up I had inwardly rebelled against the controls imposed by my parents, especially my mother. My rebellion was also resistance to the rigid and often baffling restraints of the particular brand of Catholicism I was being taught. Some time during those years, I made a vow that when I grew up I would never surrender control of my life to anyone. Many people I have met also recall making the same vow, often without being aware of it.

That night during the Al-Anon meeting, I was handed a key that opened the final lock to the mystery of my life, not from a schooled psychiatrist, a wise Guru, or even from a psychology text. My teacher had been a young man whom I would have avoided anywhere else. And I shall forever be grateful for what he taught me. The addiction I discovered in myself was not even in the books. I was— and still am, although evolving— a control addict. Later, when I recognized how nearly universal this addictive need to control is, how central it is to our ego's sense of mastery and to our own feelings of self-worth, I would call it the "Master Addiction." But there was still much more to learn about myself and this fundamental expression of unhealthy addiction.

Even a God We Can Control

One evening, a few months after the insights I gained from Trucker, a tiny, disheveled young woman named Sarah tearfully described the physical and sexual abuse she had suffered at her father's hands. She emphasized that the pain was made worse because she had always felt particularly close to her dad, more so than to her mother. He had been a minister and "everyone else thought he was perfect," she added, "but what he did cut me off from him. I felt abandoned by my daddy." In the past I would have discounted her story as having nothing to offer me. But one of my lessons from Trucker was that it is often the people whose first impression put me off who turned out to be my most valuable teachers. I gradually felt deep anger well up inside me and a strong sense of loneliness. I knew then that Sarah must be describing something that related to my own experience. But how could this be? I asked myself. I had not been abused in the ways she described. My parents had been overworked and impulsive. They were sometimes angry, and my mother, especially, lost control at times, but even her worst displays of anger hardly qualified as physical abuse. Certainly they were nothing compared to what Sarah had suffered. How then did the abuse she experienced connect with me? Why was I feeling so deeply affected?

The meeting ended and I drove away still troubled and confused. I slept restlessly that night and could not stop thinking about Sarah , but I could not connect her story to my life. Suddenly, in the early morning, I had a flash of understanding. It was not simply the abuse in Sarah's story that I had related to myself. There was something more. It was connected to her remarks about her father having been a minister and her feeling abandoned by him after the abuse. That was it. I had felt spiritually abandoned in my family. Do as our parents demanded or love would be withdrawn. Not only mother's love, but God's love as well. I had not been physically, sexually, or psychologically abused in any obvious way. My abuse had been much more subtle. When I allowed myself to focus on the inner turmoil I experienced as Sarah told her story and the confusion I felt through the night afterward, the words that came to mind, associated with my own sense of abuse, startled me.

Instead of sexual assault or the pain of physical injury, my source of abuse and abandonment had been cloaked in religious terms. Images and feelings connected with words like Heaven and Hell and Eternal Damnation came to mind. All these associations spoke to me of God. But how, I asked myself, could it possibly be that religious teachings could be abusive? How could they be the source of a sense of outrage and abandonment, like physical and sexual abuse? Had these teachings laid the foundation for my deep sense of being abandoned by God and seeking God in other ways—in unhealthy addictive behaviors?

This answer, when it finally came, seemed as obvious as it was surprising. For me, the religious teachings I had received had caused me more guilt, pain, and suffering than everything else in my life. It had undermined my ability to trust God, even as a child. I recall feeling guilty and cowardly when I heard stories about early Christian martyrs who had been tortured and slain defending their allegiance to Jesus. Later I cringed when I heard anti-Catholic sentiments in public which reaffirmed to me that I did not have sufficient faith to die for or even acknowledge my association with the God I knew. In those moments of Sarah's painful revelation my own truth began to emerge. The God of her abusive minister father and my God of my Catholic childhood were identical. That God must be man-made, created by humans, demanding standards that many of His ministers could not meet or requiring sacrifice to the point of martyrdom. This was not the God of love and peace and joy who I was discovering in those 12-Step meetings.

When I left the Catholic church, I thought I had left God. In a flash of clarity I now saw that I had not entirely abandoned my search for God at that confusing time. I had left only *that* God when I walked away from the church of my childhood. I continued to seek a substitute, something or someone I could trust and believe in totally, someone or something to take His place.

Very early in life I began seeking substitutes for my perceptions of God outside of myself—success in school and other competitions, money, recognition, flattery, relationships, any of a thousand places my ego told me I could find fulfillment. But in spite of my efforts, my spirit felt empty and without peace. That gnawing, restless inner longing always pursued me. I began to see quite clearly that what eventually became my unhealthy addictions began in childhood as a search for God. The seeds of addiction, particularly the master addiction of having to feel in control of my life, especially in relationships with others, began when my child's capacity for infinite trust and love was shattered. It was destroyed by trying to satisfy the requirements of my parents and the man-conceived God that I and Sarah and so many others of us were taught. The seeds of my later emotional breakdown, and all the other unhealthy addictive behaviors, I believe sprout from this futile search.

Sarah, who seemed to me such a sad and crumpled woman, helped me to realize this: my addictions, particularly as they were focused on feeling in control, had been attempts to find a higher power; that restless inner longing I could trace to childhood, identical to the addictive energy I later identified, was the beacon that guided me. So were the cravings of virtually everyone else I knew who was struggling with addictive behaviors. For some, of course, the sense of abuse they experienced was more violent and wrenching than mine. For others, it was a sense of profound sadness, a sense of being isolated and alone without support in the world that reflected their sense of longing and fuels their addictive search.

We all forge our own paths to escape from this judgmental and wrathful God. Numerous people I have met, many psychiatrists among them, do it by simply denying the existence of any God whatsoever. They proudly call themselves atheists. They refuse to acknowledge the existence of a Higher Power who they must win over through sacrifice and good works. Still others blunt this God's wrath by allowing themselves to be "saved," which presumably secures His love, regardless of the way they live. When we fall into this particular trap, it can become very difficult to identify our choices as addictive, and to see this God as part of our addiction. But they are, because we continue to live under layers of guilt and fear that cloud our vision. In spite of their belief that they are loved by their God or that they are "saved," I believe these people are addicted, too, to this God.

It is possible to "take the person out of the church, but not the church out of the person." Those words echoed in my brain for years before I made these discoveries. I was frequently reminded of them when, under stress, I would find myself mumbling "Hail Mary's" under my breath, or reciting other prayers that I had learned in childhood, intended to win God's favor. This judgmental God, this God of conditional love, this addictive God, died for me, not on a cross two thousand years ago, but during these 12-Step meetings, years after I had formally resigned from the church where I'd been raised.

Progress Not Perfection

Many times during the early months that I devoted to the 12-Step program I became restless and impatient. Healing wasn't going to happen over night. I approached the 12-Steps just as I had approached classes in medical school. I attacked them. I studied the Steps diligently, and I expected quick results through my obedient compliance. I wanted and fully expected packaged peace, instantly. One night at a meeting I spoke of my growing impatience. An old-timer stopped me outside after the meeting and asked, "Did you ever hear the slogan, 'Don't work the program. Let the program work you'?" I was stunned. I saw immediately that I was still trying to control. Here was that old theme in my life, only this time I was applying it to my recovery program. How subtle! I had learned the language of recovery but the process, the all-important lesson of surrender and giving up control, continued to elude me.

In my everyday life I continued to struggle, trying to control my life, though I felt I was doing it in more subtle ways than before. Eighteen months after I left my practice and moved to southern California, I returned to the San Francisco Bay area and began working again. Almost immediately, I resumed my lifelong affair with worry, preoccupied with whether or not I would ever have enough money to survive, let alone retire some day. Would the depression return and make it impossible for me to work? Did I have the fatal cancer gene which ended the lives of my three brothers? It did not take long for me to recognize the *control* theme in all these questions. I was trying to control the future as before. I realized I still had a long way to go.

The 12-Step program has a slogan which recognizes that change is often slow: "Progress, not perfection." I reflected on this truth many times as I continued my recovery.

The Power of Surrender

One night, several years after beginning recovery, I had a dream. Like most of my memorable dreams it was not complicated. And, it affected me long after I awakened:

I was alone and frustrated. I was aware that I was weary from helping everyone else. Trying to walk was nearly impossible. My arms and legs were leaden. But I continued to struggle.

A kind man appeared and began to notice my struggle. Then I became aware that the man was Lloyd Bridges, the movie actor. He motioned for me to stop and asked what I was trying to do. I stopped, feeling pleased that someone cared enough to ask about me. I felt an immediate relief, like a tremendous weight had been lifted from my shoulders. My body felt light and I could move more freely. I noted that I no longer felt alone. It was an immense comfort.

Then he began to ask about my life, which pleased me more. He seemed to know of my interest in addiction (I had already begun writing this book). He told me, "Addiction is the energy that leads us to Him." I felt excited, as if he were reading my thoughts. He pointed to himself, at his heart. Then he pointed at me. I knew what he meant, but I needed him to say it aloud. I needed someone to confirm what I already knew. "You mean God?" He just looked at me and continued to smile that sly Lloyd Bridges smile. I trusted him. I had no more questions. Once more, I felt as if a burden had lifted— this time from my mind. My head suddenly felt light. I felt at peace.

I awoke feeling contented, peaceful, and serene. The message in that dream changed my life. It confirmed what I believed but was afraid to accept without the assurances of some caring person whom I trusted. Lloyd Bridges had served me well. He was the symbol of a caring therapist, minister, or friend whose experience and wisdom I trusted. He was the bridge to a new, previously unrecognized God for me, a God of my understanding, one who dwells within me and loves unconditionally. I could end my lifelong search and acknowledge Him as I learned to acknowledge myself. We were not separate. Nor had He abandoned me; on the contrary, it was I who had abandoned Him. Years of seeking to heal my feelings of separation by trying to please a God represented in my life with human weaknesses, and later, all my addictions had blocked me from this truth. In my healing from that terrible, painful breakdown, and in the awareness of the universal nature of my addictive need to feel in control, including an addictive relationship with God, I found the answer. When I let go I surrendered to the God of my understanding.

All my earlier experiences had prepared me for this dream. I was finally able to trust again. I was able to surrender. I no longer felt either abused or abandoned. With the help of "Trucker," Sarah, my patients, Lloyd Bridges, and other teachers, I found a God whose love is unconditional, neither abusive nor capricious as the God of my childhood had been. I found God within me.

My Heart is restless until it rests in thee.

–St. Augustine

THE MEANING OF SYMPTOMS

Alcoholism. Anxiety. Burnout. Depression. Desertion. Despair. Divorce. Drug addiction. Hopelessness. Mood swings. Obsessive-compulsive rituals. Panic attacks. Phobias. Physical abuse. Sexual abuse. Emotional abuse. Sexual affairs. Excessive debt caused by shopping or gambling.

The list of symptoms of human misery and pain is nearly endless. The times we experience these feelings are frequently the lowest, most painful of our lives. Yet such times, I believe, are the most important, because these symptoms often force us to seek help. Only then do we begin to change our attitudes and beliefs, which marks the beginning of healing.

Very often it is not enough just to treat the symptoms of an illness. We can treat a headache with aspirin, but this may remove only the tip of an iceberg. Removing symptoms may lull us into believing that our inner waters are calm when indeed the bulk of the glacier remains hidden beneath our awareness. Later, like an iceberg, symptoms push upward into view and demand our attention. If we don't pay attention then, they'll continue to reappear over and over again, until we trace their origin and "melt" the source of our own disease.

Symptoms, then, carry a deeper message. Paying attention to their meaning can lead to finding their cause.

Anxiety, for example, can be quieted by any number of available medications. But anxiety is a symptom of fear. And fear is a symptom of lack of faith; of feeling alone and helpless in the universe; of an inability to truly believe and trust in ourselves, in others, or in a Higher Power. Such feelings may open the door and lead us to seek help, but they are only clues leading us to the solution of a mystery. Relieving these feelings seldom provides lasting benefit. One patient in particular taught me this lesson.

When I first saw Bernie as a patient he seemed to know as much about medication as I did—at least the drugs used to treat anxiety. He rattled off names and dosages with such authority I was amazed at first. Later on, I realized that his knowledge was based on experience. He had tried them all. He was a smallish young man with huge brown eyes. His voice cracked at the beginning of each sentence and he nervously cleared his throat every thirty seconds or so. His fear was obvious. I could feel it in the office and so I was not surprised when he admitted to having suicidal feelings.

Bernie's panic attacks had begun at a party during his junior year in high school when he tried marijuana. It was his first drug experience. And his last. He told me he felt so scared that he needed to keep everyone else at the party from seeing his fear. So he overdid it. He took a few more hits than everyone else. In a few minutes, he began to feel dizzy. His skin felt hot and crawly, and he felt that he was losing it. At first he was afraid to tell anyone; they all seemed to be having such a good time. He had read about "bad trips," and drugs mixed with other drugs; this just intensified his fear. He thought he was going crazy or would die. Finally, he just started screaming.

Fortunately two of the girls at the party were able to drive him to a hospital emergency room. The doctor on call was a close friend of Bernie's dad, who was a physician, so Bernie was afraid to admit he was on illegal drugs. Instead, he lied to the doctor and simply told him the kinds of feelings he was having, making no mention of having used street drugs. He was diagnosed as having a panic attack, given a shot, and allowed to go home. But Bernie's panic attacks continued.

Ten year later, when Bernie came to me, he was twenty-six, still having panic attacks, and still on medication. He was taking a combination of antianxiety and antidepressant medications to control his feelings. Whenever he tried to go off medication, his feelings returned. So he concluded that he needed to resume the medication.

Gradually he realized he was both physically and psychologically dependent on the drugs. He had been in psychotherapy with the same psychiatrist for many years, but their visits had grown more infrequent after the first year. Now they only met once every three months to discuss Bernie's medication. Bernie was depressed now, too, so his psychiatrist had asked him to see me.

Bernie had been a scared kid, the youngest of three sons, overprotected by his family. He had avoided taking the usual childhood and adolescent risks. His dad supported his lie that it was "allergies" that kept him from Boy Scout camp rather than his fear. In junior high he still required a night light and seemed always to have vague abdominal pains that required frequent doctor visits, though he was never hospitalized and no physical illness was ever found.

When I learned this history I was not surprised Bernie had developed panic attacks. Many overprotected kids do, later in life. The persistence of Bernie's attacks whenever he started to reduce his medication was an indicator that he was unusually fearful.

During our sessions, he became more open and truthful than he had been in the past. His pain, especially the depression, had forced him to "come off it," to be more honest. Any bravado he might have had in the past was gone, dissolved in the pain of his depression. As he told his story he began to cry softly; then he began sobbing—high-pitched child's sobs at first. Later the sobs seemed to be coming from somewhere much deeper within him. Eventually, he crawled into fetal position on the floor and his whole body trembled for a long time.

Bernie began to improve when he had the courage to face his fears. Gradually, he reduced his medication without having more panic attacks. After eighteen months, he was able to stop medication completely.

The significance of this story is that only when we started treating Bernie's painful feelings did he begin to make progress toward getting over his panic attacks. Treating only his symptoms did not reach the "core" of his emotional problems, did not touch his real feelings.

I should add here that medication is often an important part of the treatment of emotional disorders. But it only relieves painful feelings temporarily. The truth lies deeper within us than medication can reach. In fact, treating only symptoms can actually allow disease to spread, as was the case with Bernie. He began with panic attacks; later he experienced depression as well. But the attacks and depression were only the tip of the iceberg. Only when Bernie could release and face underlying feelings, long buried under a sea of confusing and disturbing experiences, was he able to begin healing.

Symptoms Are Admission Tickets for Help

Painful feelings are often "admission tickets" for help, giving people a reason to seek help without simply saying "I'm lonely," or "I'm scared, and I want you to care about me." Elderly people (defined as anyone twenty years older than we are), especially those who have been self-sufficient, are particularly vulnerable. If they have not asked for help in their younger years they are often afraid, embarrassed, and unskilled in asking for help.

Claudia worked as an executive secretary in New York until she was past eighty. She had never married. Having been the designated "dutiful daughter" from a large Italian Catholic family, she stayed home and cared for her mother until the older woman died when Claudia was seventy-four. For four years after her mother died, she comforted herself and soothed her loneliness with Johnny Walker, the Scotch companion. At seventy-eight she became the oldest member of her Alcoholics Anonymous group, which she joined after her family threatened to place her in a nursing home. At eighty-two, following the slow mend of a broken hip, she moved to California to be with her widowed sister. Her physical problems had forced her to retire, but her mind was not retired.

She was a bright-eyed eighty-three when she and her sister arrived by taxi at my office. They sat down side by side in my waiting room, obviously having just come from the hairdresser. Claudia was a near replica of the little-old-lady character played by Helen Hayes in the movie *Airport*, who smuggled herself aboard airplanes. She won my heart instantly.

Her complaints were vague. Claudia answered yes to my questions about pains throughout her body—shoulders, legs, arms, anywhere I inquired. I suspected and soon confirmed that, except for the bout of alcoholism and the hip fracture, Claudia almost never saw a doctor. She was unskilled at being a patient. Her life had revolved around herself, her mother, and her church. People like Claudia, who have little or no experience in asking for help, often answer yes to every complaint. They do this unconsciously, being able to ask for caring and support from others only in this indirect way.

It would have seemed much simpler if Claudia could have just come right out and asked for help, but she couldn't. I arranged to see her each week for several months. She responded well to support. Our chats mostly focused on her pains, because eighty-three years of prideful living had insulated her from acknowledging her need for help. Aches and pains disguised her dependency, and if their main function was to provide her with a reason to receive care from a doctor, the arrangement seemed to get her what she needed. Happily she began doing typing at the Senior Center and put a great deal of time and effort into updating their antiquated files. One day she came in for her weekly visit, and in an apologetic tone told me, "I'm sorry, Doctor, but I just don't have the time to see you anymore." We now stay in touch by phone about once a month.

Symptoms as Personal Tutors

Painful feelings can be our private tutors, our teachers, alerting us to emotions, opinions or beliefs that we have buried and suppressed. They can instruct us where we lack courage, or fear to take risks, when we try to appear as someone we are not, or attempt to control our lives beyond the point where we have control.

There are many ways to relieve pain. By medication, as in Bernie's case, or by psychotherapy, relaxation, nurturing relationships, or exercise. The pain will disappear, too, as we learn to experience our buried, unconscious feelings directly; accept them; and eventually take actions appropriate to our true feelings.

Paul had an almost constant facial twitch which began after a head-on collision that had luckily left him with only minor bruises.

The twitch began gradually after he regained consciousness. He had extensive medical and neurological exams, but no physiological cause was found. He knew the twitch disappeared when he slept.

Before he was referred to me, Paul had tried many treatments: numerous medications, various techniques of psychotherapy, hypnosis, acupuncture, mega-vitamins, and others. None of them offered him anything more than temporary relief.

When I met him, he was on medical leave from his job as a high school science teacher. He was a thick, muscular, intense young man with a deep, booming voice. His face was contorted, and the muscles on the left side of his face twitched for several seconds, then relaxed for several more. He seemed overly talkative despite his disfigurement; he continued to talk even when his face was twisted in spasm.

Through several sessions, he related minute details of his earlier life. I didn't have a clue, though, about the source of his symptom. I was soon bored. I began to feel lonely in my sessions with Paul. I felt like an object, not a person. I certainly did not feel like a trained therapist who could help, or who even wanted to.

I held to my belief that everyone should have a chance to tell his story—at least once. I let him continue his life story without interruption. My loneliness in the therapeutic relationship was my own responsibility. Yet I quickly saw that it was also a reflection of how alone Paul must feel. Finally, I could stand it no longer. I tried to sound composed when I suggested an idea that had occurred to me. I was trying to think of some way we could both survive this session, as well as help Paul. If feelings are teachers, I wanted to help Paul learn what I was learning about him and his feelings.

I asked Paul to sit quietly, continue to look at me, and imagine himself telling me what he wanted to say—but without speaking. I suggested that he experience his feelings without talking again and to observe them, allowing his inner feelings to "do whatever they want or need to do. Treat your feelings like welcome guests in your body," I encouraged him.

At first he was clearly frustrated and upset. This continued for the entire session. Each time he broke the silence, I put my finger to my lips and motioned him to remain silent. At our next meeting I was encouraged that he had returned, so I gave him the same instructions. Halfway through that session, he was perspiring, his face flushed, and his expression was one of pain and fear. His entire body began to tremble, and he resembled someone being given a series of small electric shocks. This continued for several minutes. The silence in the room was electric now. His frustration was tangible. He looked as if he were going to explode. But he remained silent.

Then he started what sounded like a growl. I was briefly afraid. He looked menacing, his eyes bulging, his face flushed and dripping with perspiration. I waited. He continued to growl, louder and deeper until he collapsed, exhausted, on my office chair. Then, surprisingly, I saw that he was asleep. His body was relaxed and his face was smooth. The twitch was gone, at least for a few minutes, until he awakened.

Over the next several meetings, I helped Paul validate and experience what he was really feeling. I made a tape recording of each session, and he listened to the tapes over and over. Once he told me that he cried for nearly two days without interruption—even while he ate and went to the bathroom. Without discussing his symptom again, Paul began to experience relief. His facial tic gradually diminished. He began to believe there was a connection between his "symptom" and his real feelings. He learned, for example, how he had resisted crying for years, and that the facial tic was an involuntary expression of his "crying muscles."

The symptom taught Paul and me what we both needed to know. I knew there was a connection yet I had no idea what it was. Paul was immersed in his symptom and his embarrassment. When he was able to let go of his fear of expressing the feelings that he associated with weakness and admit the truth of his feelings, his symptom disappeared. This was no one-time magic, like on television psychiatry (they only have one hour to cure their patients), yet it was a beginning. We now had an experience Paul and I witnessed together to help in our work.

Symptoms Disguise True Feelings

Because it is taboo in our society—and sometimes even in therapy—to express certain emotions, symptoms are a way of saving face and a way of expressing painful feelings without acknowledging them directly, as in the examples of Claudia and Paul. This is especially true for feelings we are afraid of or embarrassed to admit—so-called "weak" feelings, like dependency.

I believe this taboo is one reason we begin to ignore and disguise our inner feelings early in life. Admonitions like, "You're too big to cry!" or "Stop feeling sorry for yourself," or "I'll give you something to feel sorry about!" help to mold us, help us become afraid or ashamed to feel our feelings directly. The thought of doing so brings up the fear of being rejected, punished, unloved, or abandoned. This narrows our options, making us unbalanced in our expression of feelings. We disguise feelings, express them indirectly in ways that are acceptable, or controllable, and learn "role living" rather than real living. This is one step, I believe, toward developing "addictions."

Why Do Feelings Need to Get So Painful?

Many times patients ask, "Why did I wait so long to seek help?" "Why does it take so long to recover?" Yet we all know the answers. We do everything we can to avoid facing pain. It is not until pain becomes unbearable that we stop—stop denying, running from, tranquilizing, or somehow avoiding our pain. Actually we don't stop: we are stopped by our pain. It's pain that gets our attention, pain that forces us to our knees, and pain that finally compels us to help ourselves.

I have told patients, truthfully, that the deeper their pain, the more hopeful I feel when I begin working with them. When I see patients with frequent panic attacks, deep depression, constant anxiety, worry, or fear, I know they are closer to solving their problems than ever before. Because they are in deep pain, they are motivated to change. Pain melts defenses, pain dissolves the most stubborn egos, and pain will ultimately wipe out the barriers of denial and self-delusion that we maintain as long as we are only "uncomfortable."

We change when emotional pain or chaos forces us.

Pain forces us to look inside. When pain is severe enough, we cease looking outside for our answers.

I believe pain must become severe enough, and last long enough, to penetrate all the barriers of tradition, habit, and denial built up over an entire lifetime. Short-lived pain is seldom an adequate teacher.

For example, I frequently see patients who have been hospitalized several times for depression. The continual recurrence of their depression tells me clearly that these patients have not learned from their painful feelings. Though their pain recurs again and again, they seek relief only from medication; thus, they are unable to learn anything about the source of their pain. They resume ways of living that triggered their depression and, predictably, their symptoms return.

When pain stops us, we listen. Pain, when it becomes strong enough, can force us to look within for its source. We cease looking outside ourselves for solutions. Pain has that power. Without it, I believe most of us would never grow and change.

Stella was in agony. She was doubled over with pain in my waiting room when I met her the first time. Her large doe eyes looked innocent, yet they camouflaged a painful past—two unhappy marriages and a series of unfulfilling affairs. Now her "real love," an intimate, intense, on-and-off four-year relationship with a physician, had just ruptured. He abruptly announced that the marriage plans were off and suddenly terminated their relationship. He packed his belongings and left. Stella was devastated.

She told me she had been crying for days. Her life was mixed with hour-long spasms of grief and pain and relief. The spasms continued while we talked. For a while she would be clear, then she would touch a sensitive memory and literally double over, wrapping her chest and abdomen in a painful embrace. One particularly long spasm lasted twenty minutes.

When she finally looked up, there was a dramatic change. She suddenly seemed relaxed. She settled in the chair. Her face softened and her voice changed. She said that in her agony she had seen her dad, whom she had loved dearly. He was dying and begging her not to leave him. She had been his main support for years after her parents divorced, and though theirs was not a sexually intimate relationship, she developed a wife-like allegiance to him and had harbored guilt in every other male relationship. She suddenly realized that he had remained present in all her attempts at intimacy. She had never been free to give herself to another man. She had given herself to her dad years ago.

In her agony she had seen this. Then she began to let him go. In her deepest pain she had uncovered her buried feelings; these became the keys to her freedom. This new knowledge allowed her to unlock the door to brand new possibilities in her life.

Stella's experience is an example of the power of pain. She had been through years of therapy, with many insights. Yet she had continued the same pattern in her relationships, always saving herself for her father. Her previous psychotherapy had been more focused on understanding or explaining feelings, rather than experiencing them, giving her only temporary relief from her pain.Each insight served as a mental valium to reduce the anxiety she was feeling. Like medication, insight can temporarily tranquilize pain. Explanations can stop pain but they cannot heal the wounds.

Even long-term therapy like Stella's can fail to reach the core of the pain until we connect and experience the feelings underlying the pain. When Stella experienced her pattern, when she felt her pain, she was finally able to move beyond her feelings. She was able to begin a healing process because she came face to face with the hitherto hidden beliefs underlying her painful feelings.

Our understanding of the roles that symptoms play in our lives lets us pull aside a curtain to see through the window of truth to a larger picture than we were able to see before. In stories like Stella's and the others discussed in this chapter, we can see that there are ways of looking more deeply at our symptoms. We can uncover the beliefs that are behind them. We can make new choices in our lives.

There are many options available for coping with the pain in our lives. One of the most prevalent is unhealthy addiction. In the following chapter we'll explore exactly what unhealthy addiction is, why we choose these patterns over other ways of addressing our pain, and why it does or doesn't provide us with what we are seeking in our lives.

UNDERSTANDING ADDICTION

Addiction is not a respectable word in our language. Most of us only apply it to someone else.

Ordinarily the word *addiction* has negative connotations. We associate it with the drug war, drug abuse, and certain excesses of behavior. But becoming addicted, I learned, is not necessarily immoral and corrupting. Originally the word came from the Latin root *addictio*, meaning to "give over or surrender."

It's not the fact that we surrender to a point called addiction that makes addiction shameful and destructive. What we become addicted to does that.

Unless we have obvious, socially labeled, easy to identify, and seemingly nondestructive addictions (such as exercise, work, or computers) we apply the term *addict* to other people. I always did. I pictured an addict as someone driven by a senseless craving for booze or drugs, or a chain-smoker, or a person hooked on horse races or the craps table. Surely this word was not connected to me.

My personal experience with addiction began when I was a child. My dad, a busy salesman struggling to support mother and seven growing and hungry sons, grappled for several years with alcohol. After each binge we knew what to expect—a trip to the Monsignor at our parish followed by his signing a sincere and tearful pledge, promising sobriety. Weeks or months later he would relapse and the process would repeat. Eventually he found help in the fellowship of Alcoholics Anonymous. In fact, our family hosted the annual AA picnic at our small, summer cottage.

I was embarrassed and ashamed to tell my friends that our guests were alcoholics and their families. I was ashamed of my dad's disease and regarded him and the others as weak. I didn't want my friends to know dad was an alcoholic, or that my family was associated with "these people." Instead, I told them we were "sacrificing" (or some other noble motive) our cottage to this group for their picnic.

Even after I was a psychiatrist, I believed addictions were caused by a combination of unhealthy childhood experiences and lack of will power; they were character flaws curable by self-discipline and sacrifice (two tools Catholics of my era believed would cure anything). Deeply ingrained beliefs and pejorative judgments from my Catholic upbringing lingered. In my psychiatric training, I learned that addictions were compulsions, their causes not understood, and that talk therapy was mostly ineffective. Since we had no useful answers we simply treated the symptoms. We used drugs (supposedly to calm the underlying anxiety which "made" a person drink), or drugs that made them violently ill when they drank. Or we cautioned them and hoped that the insight of psychotherapy could help them overcome their compulsion. It never did.

"Bad" alcoholics were involuntarily committed to mental hospitals for treatment that consisted of locking them away from their booze supply as long as the law allowed. This futile, inhumane approach rarely helped, and has gradually disappeared. Today, mercifully, recognized addictions are considered more as diseases than manifestations of moral weakness, untreatable compulsions, or other pejorative labels.

There are hundreds of recognized addictions. We are constantly being exposed to new ones, usually in sensational banner headlines in the tabloids. I counted fifteen book titles about different addictions in my local bookstore on a recent tour. Anything from ancestor worship to zealot bashing has been named as an addiction.

After I accepted that I was also a member of the addiction fellowship, I began to understand the true nature of addiction. I could see that there were not many separate addictions, only many manifestations of addiction. Addictions are symptoms of an inherent human quest for fulfillment. It is possible, I concluded, to become addicted to almost anything in this quest to quiet an inner restlessness which is universal.

Addiction to our beliefs, I discovered, is at the core of all addiction. Most of us just substitute one addictive behavior for another. Alcoholics stop drinking and crave sugar. Cocaine addicts get hooked on diet sodas. And most addicts, when cut off from a familiar addictive supply, become depressed. In fact many people who come to me for help are people who have given up unhealthy addictions only to fall into deep depression, suffer panic attacks, or break down in some other way.

Defining Addiction

The most widely accepted definition of unhealthy addiction is "dependence on a chemical substance or behavior" to the extent that:

- there is a physiological and/or psychological need for that substance or behavior;
- withdrawal symptoms occur when the substance or behavior is taken away;
- there is a need for increased amounts in order to achieve the result that smaller amounts once provided (tolerance);
- behaviors, moods, states of consciousness, and emotions are affected; and
- life increasingly revolves around the habit.

These are all true statements but they fall far short of a complete definition. Addiction is much more than simply being hooked on substances or behaviors. I consider several words to be synonymous with addiction and I sometimes use them interchangeably: compulsion, craving, enslavement, and obsession.

After I first recognized myself as an addict I quickly became dissatisfied with physiological or psychological definitions. Instead I became convinced that addiction has far deeper roots than our biology or environment, and that we do not become addicted because of an addiction gene or alcoholic parent. Only the particular symptoms that we have are related to our genes and environment.

I believe that we are all addicts and that there is a meaning or purpose that our addiction serves. I firmly believe that the basic inner drive expressed through addiction is a healthy and natural one. It is an attempt to resolve problems, including dependency and quieting the restless inner energy. All addictions are efforts to express this energy as well as to find happiness, contentment, peace of mind, and serenity. This has led me to separate healthy from unhealthy additions and to distinguish our attachments and habits from addiction. In the final analysis, I am convinced that we can successfully meet the challenge of addiction only if we let go of our view of addiction as a disease and see it as a universal, inevitable part of our lives which can contribute as much to our healing as it seems to contribute to our destruction.

I believe that we grow, not by eliminating addiction from our lives, but by gradually upgrading our addictions. For example becoming addicted to 12-Step groups is an upgrade over cocaine or sex addictions. My own experience and the experiences of so many of my patients have convinced me that addiction is our ultimate problem and our ultimate solution.

It is not addiction that destroys us. Rather, the object(s) of our addiction destroy us—or they heal us.

Addiction and the Fear of Being Dependent

Addiction implies being dependent. This may sound too simple, but the major difficulty I had in accepting addiction in myself, and the major difficulty my patients have in accepting their addictiveness, is the fear of recognizing and admitting that we are truly "hooked" or dependent.

The most frequent occurrence of this that I encounter is in patients who suffer panic attacks. They are grateful for the help medication affords them (antianxiety drugs like Alprazolam [Xanax] often provide dramatic relief with the first dose), yet as soon as they feel relief, they stop taking the medication. They hate being dependent on medication, or anyone, or anything.

Their issue is the fear of admitting dependency. Many of us view ourselves as self-reliant, able to care for ourselves, and able to control our dependencies. We fiercely resist admitting dependency. But we are dependent, somewhere in our lives, even if it means we are dependent on thinking of ourselves as non-dependent.

This is also evident in my practice with patients who suffer severe depression, as I did. "I just don't want to rely on pills." If they don't express it, I can see it in their body language. They squirm or turn in their chairs when I mention medication, unless they are so depressed that their pride has been melted. You recall my statement that I had "a fool for a physician" and treated myself (or under-treated myself) for more than a year before I sought adequate professional help. I was ashamed to be dependent. I was afraid to give up control of my autonomy, even though I had lost control months, or even years earlier.

Medication is an obvious dependency. Most of us prefer subtle ones like our addiction to relationships, work, money, recognition, and power. Taking medication is a hard-to-deny and hard-to-admit dependency, not as subtle as many others. Many of my patients fear addiction to prescription drugs more than they fear any other addiction. This is often fostered by physicians and others who have not admitted their own addictiveness, who reflect their own fears about being dependent in this seemingly noble concern for patients. My personal and clinical experience has convinced me that such addictions are rarely a problem for patients who have emotional breakdowns. There are many forms of unhealthy dependency far more difficult to eliminate than the use of prescription drugs in patients who have depression, panic attacks, or other painful emotional symptoms.

The fear of admitting dependency among professionals, the shame and guilt the entire profession has in admitting to this un-holy emotion, is reflected in our treatment of patients. It affects the forms of dependency that are glorified or decried. Seeing a therapist twice a week, as long as insurance holds out, is not considered an addiction. But the long-term use of minor tranquilizers such as Xanax, Ativan, or Valium is considered addiction. Physicians, like myself, who labor in the infantry of family practice or general psychiatry, can soon decide whether our patients are using these medications for good or ill. We know that unhealthiness exists in the motives and beliefs of the patient, not in a tiny pill.

Physicians are under enormous constraints from all sides today. The constant threat of malpractice claims, the fear of criticism from our colleagues, and the constant pressure to treat patients faster and in less time, resulting from Managed Health Care, combine to drastically increase our fears. One result is that more harm has come to my patients from physicians' decisions about removing their patients from so-called addictive medications than from any possible dependence on the drugs. Judgments made on the basis of personal prejudice and unconscious fears present more danger to their patients than the pills they prescribe.

Addiction as an Expression of Energy

Addictions begin as an inner energy that is restless, constant, powerful, and compelling. It fuels the need for whatever we choose as the focus for expressing or quieting it. Traditionally in psychiatry, we refer to this energy as libido. I view it as a manifestation of our creative energy, part of our essential life force. Addictions—at least unhealthy addictions—are a misapplication of this energy; they are defined by the symptoms, the expressions of this energy in our relationships with substances or behaviors.All this is done in our efforts to control and harness this energy. Addictions are fueled by this nagging and insistent force which eventually creates panic, depression, or other symptoms of emotional breakdowns when our choice in expressing this energy fails us or leads to our destruction. Substance abuse and behavioral addictions like gambling and sex are examples of ways we express this energy in our efforts to quiet it and find satisfaction and peace.

One patient I saw in consultation, was attending seven different 12-Step groups treating her multiple addictions. She did not recognize that she was expressing her addictive-creative energy in numerous ways. What helped her was recognizing this and focusing on channeling this enormous energy in more fulfilling ways. Rather than trying to heal all her so-called addictions I helped her to focus on becoming addicted to the spiritual aspect (the God of her understanding) of the 12-Step groups. I refer to this as learning to upgrade our addictions.

Years before my breakdown, neatness was one of the most obvious outward expressions of my addictive energy. Compulsive cleaning, keeping my office and home as well as my wife and kids organized, was a near-obsession. When anything was out of order I felt a gnawing, restless uneasiness and impatience. Inner chaos, I am convinced, requires outer order. I was not aware of this at the time. I only knew I could not relax, even a little bit, unless the world around me was "in order."

This "neataholism," as I came to call it, was particularly noticeable on Sunday afternoons during the years my children were living at home. I would begin cleaning rituals that drove my family to distraction. I usually started in the garage, threw out everything that was not tied down, then made my observant rounds through the house. When all was in order, I could relax.

Now I understand that energy. It was this same addictive process in action. During the work week my energy was focused on patients and their problems. Early on weekends family activities or playing tennis absorbed my energy. On Sunday afternoon, watch out.

Compulsive cleaning was simply a form of pre-Monday jitters, common among the self-employed. It was also an expression of the creative-addictive energy. I later learned to let myself experience this without any activity and this was part of the program that helped me heal. I learned to simply feel these feelings and not act on them. My addiction wasn't to cleaning. The energy within me compelled me to clean, and when I stopped acting on this energy, a process of change began.

The energy of addiction is constantly in flux, continually changing. This is so frustrating for many of us who spend our lives hoping to arrive at a final, peaceful place where we can cease struggling, have answers, and sip healthy mint juleps or bottled water instead of struggling with our lives. There is such a state of being, often described in spiritual literature. This state is called death—death, not of the body, but of the ego. Few of us recognize this connection between our addictions and the perfect peace and contentment we are seeking.

We are seldom in any emotional state for long. Learning to be aware, accepting, and eventually grateful for the evolvement of our addictive energy as our beliefs change is part of life. It is likely that all addictions are fueled by a common energy source—FEAR. In the book *From the Heart of a Gentle Brother*, Bartholomew addresses this process in answering a question about stopping fear:

"There is only one way I have ever seen to truly stop a process and it begins with paying close attention to it, and really feeling it in your body." Further on, he says, "Fear is an energy that can be your teacher—if you have the willingness to face it."

For example, a person addicted to cigarettes or food might introduce daily exercise or a new interest, such as a computer, as substitute addictions. Or I advise attendance at 12-Step meetings with frequent calls to other members—any way to express addictive energy less destructively. Often our first steps in healing involve upgrading, replacing unhealthy addictions with more healthy ones.

As strange as it may seem, addictions are always attempts to solve problems and maintain or regain control over energy. Clearly, some addictions are more healthy than others. These upgraded addictions are referred to as "transitional addictions." They are stepping stones on the path of healing. These upgrades are not the answer but they are closer. This process can be continued, step by step, until we become addicted to a source of happiness, peace, and serenity.

Institutions of Addiction

When we attempt to recover from unhealthy addictions and redirect this energy in more healthful ways we come up against major problems in this society: many addictions have become institutionalized, part of society itself.

We can become addicted to anything our mind can conceive. Any behavior (pleasing other people); belief (self-doubt, cults, family denial systems); fantasy (fatal-attraction relationships); and endless other attachments.

Everyday habits like eating, sleeping, working, going to the bathroom, and sex all can become addictions. Recreational pursuits such as exercise, reading, television, or shopping, addict untold numbers of people. Witness the congestion in the malls or the number of televisions sets per household worldwide. Money, power, prestige, recognition, being busy, romance, goals, and even hope can all become addictions. The list is nearly endless.

Many of our social institutions profit from unhealthy addictions and thus encourage them. Our fears and inability to have choices help many businesses prosper. Advertising, for example, is constantly directed at our fears and insecurities by promising to satisfy our addictions.

We are encouraged by youthful, fun-loving, vibrant, attractive people to do as they seem to be doing and buy automobiles, smoke cigarettes, or use proffered deodorants. We then associate that product with those qualities. The message of this advertising is that these beautiful people got that way because they used the products being offered.

Have you noticed that shopping malls and gambling casinos never have clocks in evidence? That's no accident. They want people to be oblivious to time. Shopping malls provide attractive, seductive, easily obtained objects for our addictive energies. "We give instant credit!"

The military establishment, in this post-cold-war era, survives and flourishes on an appeal to our addictive fears of being overwhelmed and out of control to a faceless enemy depicted in the media.

The life insurance and investment businesses thrive on our addiction to security and our fears of being elderly, alone and impoverished.

Even established religions pander to our addictive fear of death and the hereafter by selling salvation. Addictive lures are everywhere.

Recovery from unhealthy addictions is not easy even under the best circumstances. It is more difficult when an entire society glamorizes various addictions with advertisements and expectations that undermine attempts at recovery.

This is one reason support groups like Alcoholics Anonymous and other 12-Step recovery programs are essential. Because of the

~~continual allure promised in the "eat, drink, and spend freely" cul-~~ ture we inhabit, few addicts maintain sobriety without continuing support. This explains why maintaining attendance at meetings is so often essential.

We are fragile. All of us. I believe recovery from unhealthy addictions requires that we surround ourselves with like-believing people to overcome the pressures which draw us like stretched rubber bands back to our former unhealthy, addictive ways. We need continuing help and support to remain clear.

Many who know me have heard me say how important changing my lifestyle was when I began recovery. I admitted my weakness, limited my work, and vigorously avoided some of my former friends who remained addicted to wealth, materialism, and getting rich, which I discovered had been a focus of my addictive energy (though I was never very successful in achieving wealth). I found myself again thinking in the language of materialism if I spent more than a friendly lunch with them. I learned to respect my fragile nature. I could feel the recently quieted surges of energy beginning again. I could recall my lengthy depression with its seemingly endless pain. Then I could graciously withdraw and once more join the stumbling, struggling mass of people devoted to recovery.

Addictions as Attempts to Find Solutions

Addictions have characteristics which go deeper as we attempt to quiet our restless inner energy. Addictions are answers, even though wrong ones, to problems. Addictions are an attempt to fix or avoid pain, unwanted feelings, emotions, feared experiences—anything we prefer to avoid.

Addictions are always attempts to get too much (love, comfort, pain relief) from too small a source of supply. What are the problems we typically try to solve by adopting unhealthy addictions?

1. Feelings of Loneliness or Powerlessness

Addictions serve as temporary companions. I hesitate to say friends because many addictions are painful, but not at first. When we act addictively we have company. We are not alone. We feel in control. The pain of being alone or feeling vulnerable and helpless ceases to exist, at lease for a time. Guilt from past failures, or our fear of what lies ahead disappear if only for as long as the substance, the behavior, the belief, or the companion we attach to lasts. When it fades, we are alone again with our pain. We are back to being the same person who feels inadequate or in some way flawed. And the process continues.

2. Escape from the Past and the Future

When we act upon addictive energy, we experience temporary relief, excitement, or brief satisfaction. We are unaware of pain until the experience is over. We are absorbed in the moment. The past and future (where pain lies) do not exist. Even painful addictions (like bulimia with compulsive eating followed by vomiting) produce an initial rush, followed by pain. We can begin now to understand why people repeat behaviors that have not worked before but serve as a temporary, family, distraction.

3. Filling the Void

When we cease any addiction, we experience a feeling of emptiness for awhile. It is an unfamiliar feeling, not always deeply painful, often just vaguely uncomfortable. We are not used to the experience of being alone, without the buffer that our addiction provides. This may be called restlessness, boredom, uneasiness, loneliness, or withdrawal. We may long for the addiction even when we know it was destroying us. When we stop our addiction we leave a void to fill—a hollow, empty, painful, unfamiliar place inside us. It may be a void of time, previously spent indulging our addiction. Or it may be absence of the momentary power or pleasure we felt when we were doing our addictive thing.

4. Self-Nurturing

Addictions, including those that result in emotional disorders, stem from attempts at self-nurturing. No one chooses the pain of addiction. Addictions don't start out as attempts to create misery and uncontrollable attachments.They begin as attempts to provide comfort, relief, change of pace, pleasure, or enjoyment. We choose them in our attempts to avoid pain and feel better, to provide a sense of being cared for that we believe we can get in no other way.

5. Returning to Familiar Pain

Addictions are like rubber bands. When we stretch ourselves to change addictive habits, they pull us back to return to that habit because of its familiarity. Our brains and bodies are grooved. People in recovery programs wisely do not ever refer to themselves as *recovered*. They are always *recovering*. They recognize the appeal of the familiar—the attraction to quiet pain in familiar ways (even though painful and proven destructive). It is a seductive lure to seek relief and satisfaction in old addictive habits just one more time.

Even when addictions are more positive, they have a quality that is always dangerous: they take control of our lives. For example, although, physical exercise is positive and healthy, doing excessive aerobics can produce physical stresses on the body and harbor many addiction-related problems. Steroids used by weight lifters and the runner's high can lead to complications both physical and emotional when the activity or usage is taken to the extreme—where the rubber band is stretched to the breaking point.

I love to watch the annual triathalon race from Hawaii—a grueling competition that combines a 2.4-mile swim, a $100^{\pm}$ mile bike ride, and a 26-mile marathon run. Watching the superb physical conditioning of the participants, I feel a certain envy as I pat my own soft belly. Indeed, the participants' lives—including their moods, states of consciousness, and emotions—obviously revolve around the conditioning program. For many, the overall result is positive because this activity leads to increased self-esteem which improves and enhances their lives.

For some, however, the competition gradually becomes as unhealthy as alcohol. It results in self-centeredness, depression, and isolation—three of the most common features of unhealthy addiction.

In my practice, I have seen people addicted to physical exercise. I've seen athletes destroy their legs with too much exercise. I have seen the onset of suicidal depression when exercise is restricted because of illness or injury.

Sonny was forty-five and had competed several times in Iron Man marathons ranging from 50 to 100 mile distances. His evenings and weekends were spent running. He kept logs of his runs, detailing his fatigue, his pain, and his times. One Sunday afternoon, he injured his knee in a bike mishap and could no longer run distances. He was referred to me because of the severe depression he experienced when he could no longer practice, let alone compete. His depression was relieved quickly by medication, but a second surgery left him stiff in one knee. He sued the driver of the car that hit him. Next, he wanted to include the surgeon in the suit. He remained restless and agitated. He required two stays in a closed psychiatric unit because of his and my fears that he would harm himself or someone else.

Sonny was able to get over his severe depression through a program designed for recovery from substance abuse. He returned to work and accepted moderate exercise using a huge brace on his knee.

Why Willpower Cannot End Addictions

We cannot overcome addictions by willing them away. The addictive process is not under conscious control.

Most weight loss programs, for example, are based on a belief that overeating is an issue of knowledge about food and will power and that it is under our conscious control. If we have the right combination of food, information, and support, we can maintain sexy slimness. Well, it doesn't work, because few programs of this kind address the underlying roots of the problems we attempt to solve with overeating.

People who frequently diet learn that each new diet is less effective, more difficult to maintain, and the results last a shorter time. Today, nutritionists tell us there are physiological reasons for this as well as psychological and spiritual ones. Theories of weight loss (except for Overeaters Anonymous) imply that addictions and addictive energy can be controlled. They can—but only for a while.

We see this same belief operating in psychiatric disorders. Panic, depression, obsessive-compulsive rituals and phobias are viewed as being unconsciously motivated. The assumption is that when the unconscious motives become conscious, when we understand them and know what caused them, we can control them. Again, the belief is that we can will these conditions away once we understand them.

Emotional disorders, I believe, are based on addictions too; they are addictive beliefs and are not under conscious control. Recovery cannot be willed for these any more than it can for alcoholism. Addictive energy, as we have seen, simply reattaches elsewhere—addictively.

Like many Catholics and former Catholics I struggled mightily with guilt about petting (defined as "everything but...") and masturbation as a teenager and young adult. Extramarital sex was out of the question in those pre-birth-control-pill years among most of my equally Catholic peers, so we petted and masturbated to express our sexuality. I doubt this habit would fit my present definition of addiction, but in those years I considered it to be a mortal sin (one which would earn me Hell fire if I died unforgiven). No matter how much I willed myself to stop, I continued to be sexual, even though it had embarrassing consequences.

If I did not confess my "sin" to a priest in confession before receiving communion, I could not partake because I was not in a state of grace. Since almost any sexual expression (including thoughts) was a mortal sin, I was guaranteed a trip to Hell if I died unforgiven. I frequented confessionals for years.

Picture our family kneeling together at Sunday Mass. The time for receiving communion arrives and I do not accompany the others to communion. Instead, I remain in the pew, head down, appearing to pray reverently. Inside I feel awful because I know what is going to happen later. As soon as we leave church, mother asks, "Why didn't you receive communion, Phil?" (Dad never asks. He knows why.) Since the church laws then required complete fasting from food and liquid from midnight prior to receiving communion, I would answer, "I forgot and drank water after midnight."

I learned very young that willpower cannot cure addiction.

Addictions as Idols or False Gods

Addiction makes a god of anything that is not God. Addictions become idols or false gods created by our needs. They become more central, more important than anyone or anything else in our lives. We empower a substance, an activity, a belief, an attitude, a group or a person with the time, energy, and power that spiritual people devote to their God. These are more than temporary nurturing companions in time of need; addictions reach much deeper and further within us and can become our deities. They become a way of life.

We give our addictions first priority in our lives. We pay homage to them, serve them. They do not serve us, except for a very short while, even positive or health-improving addictions. Addiction, then, is making a god out of anyone or anything that is not God.

Why Psychiatry Cannot Cure Addictions

I have never known an alcoholic who recovered using psychotherapy alone. I have seen many stop drinking, but many more who died from complications of alcoholism. No one in my experience recovered and lived a more fulfilling life unless the addictive substance or behavior, was stopped a profound inner awakening or transformation occurred, often with the help of psychotherapy.

One patient, Celia, was fifteen when we first met. She was the adopted daughter of a prominent local politician and his socialite wife. She was hooked on alcohol and amphetamines and had tried every other drug available during her era—LSD, nitrous oxide (laughing gas), and marijuana. Her life was clearly out of control when her parents picked her up at the police station where she had spent the night charged with drunk and disorderly conduct in a public place. This was only one in a series of embarrassing jail tours for Celia.

When I saw her parents' faces I thought she would prefer my office—no matter what I turned out to be like—to being around them. They looked defeated, but not enough to hide their anger, hurt, and embarrassment. Celia's eyes were bloodshot but blazing when she turned toward me after sitting stiff-backed and silent, facing away from me for several minutes after she reluctantly accompanied me from the waiting room.

"I suppose you're going to give me one of those lectures like the social worker at Juvenile Hall," she taunted me. I said nothing. I had been in similar situations enough times to know that's exactly what I had to offer Celia—nothing. Certainly no advice. I could see she was prepared for the worst. Everything about her, her flaming red hair, her flushed face, her body language, shouted, "Butt out of my life!" I was certain she had seen lots of people, unwillingly, in the two years since she became "incorrigible," the term used in the 1970s to describe young people who wouldn't comply to authority.

"This is not going to help!" she shouted. I doubt if she knew that she had voiced a prophecy. How accurate she was! But I tried everything I had to offer—individual and group therapy; family sessions; in-patient care; consultations with her school, the probation department, and other specialists seeking to help this chaotic young woman and her family. Finally in desperation her family removed her from my care, and Celia was admitted to an Alcohol and Drug Rehabilitation Center. She hated that too. She was drunk the evening of her discharge a month later.

Unsuccessful patients are easy to forget. Somehow, though, I couldn't forget Celia. She stuck in my mind. Over and over I thought about what I could have done differently—or better. I was pleased several months later when I noticed on my calendar we were scheduled to meet that afternoon.

I hardly recognized Celia when I saw her. She was completely changed. Her face was radiant and her striking red hair was cut in short bangs which gave her a pixie-like look. I had never noticed her dimples before—probably because I had never seen her smile. She said she had been clean and sober for eighty days and wanted to thank me for trying so hard. She also wanted to offer amends for her behavior months ago when we had struggled to be patient and psychiatrist. She told me she had, "found the Lord" at a spiritual center where she had spent eight weeks and was active in 12-Step Recovery. As she sat opposite me all I could think about, were the hours I had spent with Celia and all the other professionals who had been involved in her care. My pride was wounded. I inwardly questioned her change, her motives, and her answer. But she remained sober and began seeing me regularly for psychotherapy. After she was clean and sober, she grew steadily and was able to graduate with her classmates and begin college.

In 1972, shortly after I began using the "feel your feelings" therapy, I had an even more dramatic and frustrating experience which finally convinced me of the inadequacy of psychiatry and psychotherapy alone for treating patients with addictions.

I witnessed patients changing rapidly as they practiced this approach. Many seemed to experience resolution of deep problems. Changes (now called "healing the inner child") were far more evident and more lasting than in any therapy I had practiced before. Those earlier changes, in encounter groups, for example, required the support and energy of other group members. The changes never remained for long after the groups ended. No one could bottle group energy and consume it as needed in everyday life.

The process of feeling your feelings seemed so powerful. And each person became his or her own therapist. I believed this was the way to transformation.

Teri was the youngest daughter of one of the wealthiest and most influential families in southern California. Her grandfather, one of the earliest settlers there, had acquired a vast real estate empire which was gradually being developed by his heirs. Teri had the gift and the burden of wealth, recognition, and nearly unlimited opportunity and choices. She was tall, blonde, intelligent, and strikingly attractive except for a two- inch scar on her forehead (her face had struck the windshield of her sports car when she drove off the road during her senior year of high school while "blotto drunk.")

I had seen her briefly during the time of her accident, but she had left the area to attend design school and I lost track of her. Two years later her family called me and asked if I would see her. She had dropped out of school when she totalled her second sports car on a bridge in Beverly Hills. Debris from her car had seriously injured a pedestrian. A lawsuit had already been filed against her. She was drinking at the time and taking amphetamines. After a brief time in jail, her family heard about her plight and bailed her out. She was tearful and distraught when we met. Teri was facing unknown legal consequences, and her family was at a loss to understand that she could not simply stop drinking or using drugs.

Her blue eyes were red from crying and she dabbed at her eyes throughout much of our first interview. She had been seeing a well-known psychotherapist in Los Angeles during the time she was in school there and she had learned the language well. She explained her feelings of not being able to live up to family expectations, the pressure she was under because of her privileged background, and how one failure set her up for the next. She understood her addiction. Despite her expensive therapy, she was unable to stop.

I recommended that she live at the residential center I had set up for people to do process. I wanted her to feel her feelings. I believed her other therapists had simply helped her to understand her feelings and thus she had not become desensitized to them. I concluded, according to my theory then, that whenever she had strong feelings she drank rather than experiencing them. I believed she could face her feelings; I believed this process was her answer.

Three days after she started the program I discovered Teri drunk. She had concealed a hidden supply of alcohol and drugs at the center. She had never stopped drinking or taking amphetamines. I had been too naive about alcohol addiction and too enamored of my therapy program to notice. Embarrassed, I called her family and they wisely admitted Teri to a lengthy program at a drug and alcohol recovery center. After two more years of sobering up and relapsing she stopped drinking and using drugs.

The experiences with Celia and Teri were painful and humbling for me. They began my own change. I learned several lessons. First, unhealthy addictions are primary disorders which must be treated before underlying emotional problems can be addressed. Psychiatry, even the methods I offered Teri, could not effectively treat addictions. Secondly, programs like Alcoholic Anonymous and other spiritual programs are an important if not essential part of recovery. Solutions for addictions, I concluded, lie beyond the scope of what I learned and practiced as a psychiatrist. As you can tell this was many years before I realized that psychiatry is ineffective in treating addictions and that I, too, am an addict.

Is It Addiction or Attachment?

We all have people, places, and things in our lives to which we are attached. Routines. Methods. Systems. Preferences. These can be obvious or subtle. Are these addictions? If not, what are the differences between ordinary attachments, habits, likes and dislikes, and addiction? Whether we consider any of these addictions depends, I believe, on two main factors:

- whether or not we have a choice;
- whether or not we have balance.

Having a choice to do or not do anything, comfortably, implies that we have an attachment and not an addiction. It is the presence or absence of *choice* which differentiates attachment and addiction.

Attachment implies we can give it up without much effort and without withdrawal symptoms.

Balance is related to choice. It implies moderation, being able to set limits or walk away. It's a grey area (rather than black or white), it means having opinions.

Attachment to work or a hobby, for example, can become a temporarily useful addiction after a spouse dies or following a divorce. Attachments, in my experience, do not automatically grow into unhealthy addictions as some fear. Many people become absorbed in activities, but when their lives change so do their activities. These are not true addictions.

My own attachments begin in the morning with reading the newspaper and end at night with listening to the eleven-o'clock news. Yet I ask myself "do I have a choice?" If I do (yes, I still do!), then I am not addicted. The degree of choice and balance that we have are the factors that separate a harmless attachment or habit from unhealthy addiction.

Many times people who are addicted deceive themselves and others. They believe falsely that they are in control, that they have a choice. Alcoholics, gamblers, or people in compulsive relationships frequently say they can quit. They believe it is true. People in recovery recognize this as the denial stage of addiction.

When Habits Become Addictions

As a child I often heard my mother say: "Sow a thought and you reap an act. Sow an act and you reap a habit. Sow a habit and you reap an eternal destiny." Within the context of my family's religious beliefs this statement was grim and formidable. Later, within the context of recovery, it went through a transformation.

I learned from recovery that sowing thoughts, acts and habits is more complex than deciding to do so. Habits can be helpful or destructive depending on the degree to which we have balance and choice in them. Many habits reflect my favorite expression: "Our greatest strength is always our greatest weakness." Going back to my addiction to organization and neatness, I am happy to report that these have become assets. Being organized helps me simplify my living and accomplish many things that I enjoy. Yet for years it was addictive. I had no balance and little choice. What's the difference?

Today, my neatness is a good habit that I developed and groomed for years. In my prerecovery years it was an expression of my addictive energy because I felt the I had to be neat. I found the restlessness and agitation unbearable when I was not.

I am not cured. Sometimes compulsive feelings return, but now it is a habit and not an addiction. This is further evidence that unhealthy addictions and recovery from them is a continuing process not a single event.

When Unhealthy Addictions Turn Into Healthy Ones

I believe unhealthy, self-defeating addictions are often a necessary step in the process of healing a wound that we may initially not even know is there. We experience life so much in contrasts. We appreciate daylight because of darkness, warmth because of cold, summer because of winter, and health because of illness. Eventually, we appreciate healthy addictions in our lives because of our experiences with unhealthy ones.

Whatever the addiction, anyone who bottoms out (and this includes people with emotional problems such as panic attacks, phobias, depression, obsessive thoughts or compulsions), can appreciate the happiness, contentment, peace and serenity that healing brings. The pain that was felt before healing provides a contrast that few people ever forget.

Addiction can become our healer when it is focused and directed in a place that satisfies my criteria for a healthy addiction—nearly continuous happiness, contentment, peace and serenity. This is a healthy addiction.

Transcending Our Addictions Together

Experiences with patients like Celia and Teri and so many others taught me that each patient-psychiatrist relationship is one in which both patient and doctor are learning. Psychiatrists are not simply teachers; often our life experience is far too limited for us to be valuable teachers, at first. We are always students too.

Psychiatric theories and treatment tools are too limited to reach the deep, painful inner core of addiction. We can only help others grow as far as we have grown. As psychiatrists we can only share our knowledge and life experience. If we recognize and accept these facts, we will continue to grow. For this reason, if no other, I have been humbled by my patients. They who have been my mirrors have helped me grow beyond my own early experience. Our combined experiences have helped us all move past the limits of psychiatric theory—much further than I ever envisioned.

The search never ends. Yet for me, acceptance of myself as the student of my students, the patient of my patients, as well as their teacher, remains a monumental marker on my journey.

Throughout the journey of recovery, of freeing ourselves to enjoy lives of serenity, we are guided from within by our own feelings. How we make use of this valuable source of guidance is the subject of the next chapter.

THE LANGUAGE OF FEELINGS

Feelings are our internal instruction manual, written in a language which is universal. Heeding them can teach us truths about ourselves far beyond what we can learn from any other source.

Within each of us is this innate manual for living our lives. This manual is written in the universal language of feelings. Acting as our own inner guidance system, it contains answers to every question we might have about our goals, aspirations, and purpose. Heeded, this guidance system is a wonderful combination of trustworthy friend, the voice of our inner child, our most faithful lover, and our wisest teacher. Unheeded, the same messages that we might find within its pages can bring us down, causing disease. We find that when we ignore the guidance of our feelings we endanger our lives just as surely as the unheeded instructions contained in a new car manual can bring damage to the machine or our selves.

Feelings are our body's monitor and temperature gauge, reflecting each change in our thoughts and attitudes. Recognized and listened to, feelings can guide us to our beliefs. This combination of feelings and beliefs is our most solid guide to the answers to life's most essential questions. I believe their energy is the same energy that fuels unhealthy addictions, including our emotional breakdowns. Healing occurs when we follow the instructions of our inborn guide back to health.

Feelings express a language which is universal. This language conveys the joy of success as well as the pain of failure and illness. Feelings of happiness in the frigid northern plains of Siberia are indistinguishable from those same feelings in sunny California. So are feelings of anxiety, panic, and depression. They declare themselves so clearly, in a nonverbal way, that words are not necessary to recognize them.

Feelings are most easily available to us as small children. Plato seems to have recognized this when he said, "life is a forgetting." In adulthood, reestablishing our connection with our feelings involves removing the barriers we have erected to protect ourselves from pain. As a result of being battered by life's experiences, most of us toughen. We lose easy access to feelings. This loss leaves us with questions such as "Who am I?"

Happy children never ask such questions. They are too busy living to reflect on life. Too busy being. They are not so involved in doing as many of us adults. As a result, most children know who they are. They retain access to their feelings until they are required to disguise, deny, or bury them in order to be loved—or, in worst case scenarios, to simply survive abusive treatment by parents, siblings, or peers.

Separation from feelings began early for most of us. During my depression, I could trace my awful sadness to childhood. When I consider my own children, it seems they did not exhibit any lasting sadness when they were allowed to just be what they were—children. Many of my patients can trace the beginnings of their fear and depression to experiences they had as kids. Eventually these feelings lock in. They become buried and we learn to live as if we feel okay. When breakdowns occur we can no longer fake happiness. Once painful feelings are unburied and experienced ("feel your feelings, don't act on them"), happier ones can then be recalled, and experienced too. In order to heal and restore ourselves we use this link, this "feeling connection" as our healer.

During my breakdown and healing I stopped being concerned with other people for the first time in my life. The noises inside me were so loud that I had no energy to pay attention to anyone else. Later I realized the wisdom of my feelings. They forced me within, where I was at last able to begin changing lifelong patterns of separating myself from my feelings. I realized I was so addicted to looking outside for solutions that only the power of a breakdown could overcome the strength of my compulsive habit to look "out there" for my answers.

I recall not caring about others' feelings for the first time in my life, apart from times when I had a few drinks or was surrounded by supportive friends. I could go to the store, a restaurant, or, to the hospital, and not be charming and conversational. It was not a happy solution. It was like a pendulum swinging into the opposite side of its arc. Before, I compulsively communicated. Now I was unable to communicate. The instructive thing about it was that I could see, for the first time in my life, that the world could get along quite well on its own, regardless of whether I interacted with it or not. It did not depend on me; on the contrary, I realized I had been dependent on it. This was an important beginning for me. It was a step toward having choices. It was a step away from my unhealthy addictions.

What Are Feelings?

Over the years of searching I spent many hours reflecting on that question: What are feelings? I came up with some definitions that have served me well. Feelings are body energy accompanied by physical sensation. I see feelings as more inclusive than emotions. Love and hate are feelings and emotions. Physical pain is a feeling, but not an emotion. Feelings include any sensation recognized by one of the five senses that we can point to. It is noticeable and has a particular location. Even when my patients protest that they feel "nothing," they can point to where "nothing" seemingly exists. Even nothing is a feeling.

First of all feelings are *energy*. We know this best because they are constantly changing. We can recognize the changes. Never are we able to "hold on" to feelings. And they are always accompanied by a *physical sensation*. We can point to feelings. Fear, for example, is experienced in the gut, chest, or throat areas; anger throughout the chest,

throat, arms, and hands; love in the heart area; passion in the geni-
tals. These energy areas are called *chakras* in Eastern systems of
thought, where one's personal development is seen in terms of bringing balance to each of these centers. This is a process that involves
our feelings.

Feelings arrive, stay for a while, even if it seems like forever, then
disappear. But no feeling lasts forever.

Often we are not aware of our feelings' origins or why they came
to be. They arise from experiences and beliefs from childhood which
reflect our view of ourselves, other people, and our world. Most of us
begin life as a clear screen, free of impressions, opinions, attitudes, or
judgments. Directly and indirectly, we are taught how to look at and
interpret our world. Our feelings reflect what we learned. We believe
what we are taught to believe. And our feelings mirror our beliefs.

Feelings, I am convinced begin with beliefs. Changing beliefs
alters those feelings.

Since feelings reflect our beliefs, they have no life of their own. So
there cannot be true or false, right or wrong, good or bad feelings.
Feelings have no morality. Feelings are neutral. False beliefs have
taught us differently. Some feelings (pleasant or "pleasing" ones) are
considered okay. Others (fear, anger or resentment) are not. Treating
feelings—which only reflect our beliefs—as if they had lives of their
own leads to confusion about them being right or wrong, acceptable
or unacceptable. More than that, treating feelings as if they had autonomy frequently leads to years of painful shame, embarrassment, and
guilt. This confusion comes about when we ourselves are confused
about beliefs and feelings, and we raise our children to believe that
there are "bad" feelings that must be disguised or denied.

Feelings cannot be controlled. We can only control whether or
not we act on them. They seem to arrive on their own, triggered by
beliefs that we may not even realize we have. Suddenly we are feeling sad, angry, or afraid. Or happiness might arrive for "no reason"
that we can immediately discern. We can try to change or get rid of
feelings, but most often we cannot. Their conditions do not include
that we can will them away.

We can control whether or not we take action on feelings. We can
choose between "feeling feelings" or "taking action" on them. Devel-

oping the ability to recognize and make this choice is a central focus of healing. Remember that feelings contain energy, and when we give ourselves permission to feel them we provide the opportunity that allows this energy to dissipate and be released.

Being steeped in a need for perfection I recall the surge of "energy" I experienced whenever I was criticized. Like most perfectionists I avoided any risks. It was my way of avoiding criticism and the ensuing embarrassment, defensiveness or anger, all of which I found painful. When feelings are simply felt rather than acted upon, the inclination to act that follows allows the energy to slowly go away. This is one of the conditions of feelings.

Feelings cannot be forced or produced on demand.

I recall Giorgio, a warm, caring, sensitive Italian veterinarian, who had returned home after six months of separation from his wife Claudia. Claudia was a beautiful, equally sensitive woman who had grown up in a cold and rejecting home. She had never learned (or had permission) to express affection, so she was unable to nurture Giorgio during their more than twenty years of marriage. He felt too responsible for Claudia's pain after he left, and too guilty in displeasing his unhappily married parents to remain separated from her, in spite of his discontent. Yet, when he came home, he felt no love or affection for Claudia. He worked diligently to feel love for her.

He arrived at one of our sessions with a long list of affirming sentences like "I truly love Claudia," written over and over, followed by "I want to be her loving husband," recorded as many times. Yet he felt nothing but anger and emptiness.

Once set in motion within us feelings are like the flow of a river. They have their own source, their own course and direction. And like swimming in a river we learn our best choice is not to try and "push the river," but to "go with the flow." For Giorgio, he found that his answer was neither in staying or leaving. His answer was within his feelings. He could not force himself to feel love. When he felt nothing for Claudia, it was the beginning of his healing. His feelings were his truth. Feeling nothing and trying to feel love meant to him that his relationship was not working. Instead he learned to trust his feelings. Feeling nothing for Claudia was the beginning of Giorgio's journey within. He learned that in order to love and be loved by others, he must first feel love for himself.

Feelings are to be "felt," not understood.

My life and practice changed dramatically when I read Arthur Janov's first book, *The Primal Scream*. My training and my earlier experiences in psychiatry, taught that we helped patients understand feelings. Supposedly, it was enough to just know. Janov and others began teaching that we must experience our feelings. This is a most important difference. Understanding is just another form of tranquilizer. This "mental valium" may calm emotions temporarily but it does not lead to permanent change. I would often tell patients who asked "why do I feel this way?" that if I offered them an interpretation, it would help them "only as long as it takes you to get from my office to the freeway," which is a distance of about two miles.

Even feeling "nothing" is a feeling. It is not possible to be completely feeling-less. If we are aware, we are feeling. Even awareness is a feeling. Many "thinkers," who rely heavily on concepts and ideas, find it difficult to grasp this concept. I recall a brilliant professor who seemed puzzled by my definition of feeling. Finally, I asked, "Professor, do you know what you experience when you have to urinate?" He did. "That," I told him, "is a feeling." He began to understand.

Feelings are intended to be experienced. Feelings are similar to muscles. They develop from use. If we avoid feelings, beginning in childhood, they resemble the muscles of "couch potatoes"— weak, flabby and easily overwhelmed. Muscles need exercise; feelings need to be experienced. Just as weight training develops strength and endurance in muscles, so "feeling our feelings" develops strength and endurance in feelings.

The purpose of feelings is not to be understood, but felt. Feeling feelings is a skill which can be learned.

Feelings are to our bodies what sunshine, clouds, wind, and sudden changes are to the weather. They are the outer manifestations of either inner bliss or chaos, love or fear. Their outcome and direction are sometimes difficult to unravel, but their power cannot be controlled or ignored. Just as we can learn to read the skies and predict what weather lies ahead, we can learn to turn inside and search out the meaning behind our painful feelings and "dis-cover" (remove the cover from) the source of our own disease.

We begin dis-covering our feelings by feeling them. But we get to their sources by looking at the beliefs that give them form. These beliefs are our keys to self-knowledge, change, and personal growth. What they are and how we can work with them is the subject of the next chapter.

THE POWER OF BELIEFS

Dramatic healings have occurred throughout history. Healings occur using quite diverse methods. Today we are beginning to understand the biochemistry of belief, and such miracles no longer seem so mysterious. The power of belief is once more fashionable, because science can begin to explain it.

My kids like to remind me of all the words of wisdom I offered them when they were growing up. The one they most often mention is my query, "Who said life was fair?" I pulled this one out whenever their sibling bickering exceeded my tolerance. Whenever I intervened, my way of settling disputes seldom pleased everyone; there was always someone who cried plaintively, or in some cases defiantly, "It isn't fair!" After a while they didn't even wait for my reply. They would turn and walk away, muttering, "I know, I know—who said life was fair?"

I used to wonder where they learned to expect that life was fair in the first place. It must have been from their mom and me because we didn't hire any surrogate parents in those years, and most of our relatives were across the country, so we can't blame them. Most likely it was included in the "You Must Learn to Share" course that parents teach their children. This carries with it the implication that sharing is "fair," which gradually evolves into "my way is the fair way."

By the time we reach school our beliefs are firmly rooted and our expectations of ourselves and others are well established. Life becomes a series of events wherein we play out our beliefs, and our expectations are either met or frustrated. We live, and sometimes die, by our beliefs.

The Power of Belief

If I asked you what the most powerful system in the human body was, what would you answer?

The musculoskeletal system with its sinewy musculature? The nervous system with its ability to connect and integrate millions of cells in the body at astonishing speed? Perhaps the cardiovascular system which carries nourishment to every cell in the body continuously throughout our life? Or possibly the immune system which provides such elaborate barriers against disease?

It may surprise you to discover that the most powerful system in our bodies, the one that controls all these other systems, is actually the *belief system*. More than anything else, more than what we eat or drink or feel, we are what we believe. Beliefs we have about ourselves and our lives affect us at every level, from how healthy or unhealthy we are physically to how successful or unsuccessful we become in our chosen careers.

Proof of the power of our beliefs has been around for centuries but in recent times it has become the focus of much medical research. There is increasing scientific evidence that beliefs profoundly affect every bodily system, but particularly the immune system, which influences our resistance to illness and our ability to heal. For example, we now know that healthy beliefs unleash powerful chemicals called neuropeptides (protein-like substances) in the body, which facilitate healing. These natural chemicals have been found in almost every organ in the body.

Beliefs Can Heal

One of my favorite stories about the power of belief involves the study of some twenty-five women from a farming community in Idaho. They were diagnosed as having cancer and given gloomy prognoses by their doctors. Many of them showed amazing healing despite these dire medical predictions. When asked about this remarkable turn around, many of the women replied, "We have been used to government agriculture experts telling us about farming all our lives, and they were usually wrong. Doctors are no different to us than those other so-called experts."

Many other accounts of spontaneous remission of serious illness abound. There are numerous documented cases of people who were diagnosed by doctors as having incurable diseases, but when they immersed themselves in the waters of Lourdes, France, they were miraculously healed. These cures defy scientific explanation.

In addition, there are many books detailing the healing powers of laughter, prayer, or special diets. And there are accounts of miracles, unexplained recoveries, and mysterious cures in every language, and on every continent.

There is one common ingredient in all of these miraculous cases: *belief*.

A current best-selling, self-help book by Dr. Wayne Dyer bears the title *You'll See It When You Believe It*. It is just one more example of the growing recognition and acceptance of the power of belief. Books like this one are important beginnings. They help us—especially those of us who were trained in science and are aware of its limitations—to become conscious of the powerful effects of beliefs.

However, in his book, Dr. Dyer assumes we are in complete control of our beliefs and can change them through the exercise of "will." My experience with my own and patients' beliefs and addictive natures leads me to believe that simply knowing about our beliefs and willing them to change is not enough. If it were, excellent self-help books, such as the ones Dr. Dyer writes, would be all that we would need to make desired changes in our lives.

Beliefs Can Kill

While our beliefs can heal, they can also kill.

One example, described in Dr. Blair Justice's book *Who Gets Sick*, involves a fourteen-year-old girl who dropped dead when informed of her seventeen-year-old brother's unexpected death. Dr. Justice, a psychologist, carefully researched the medical literature and makes a clear, well-documented case for beliefs affecting our illness and healing. He emphasizes how feeling hopeless and lacking a sense of control affects the outcome of any disorder.

Dr. Curt Richter, at Johns Hopkins, studied the profound effects of beliefs. He was the first to describe the "giving up" reaction in rats who were placed in situations where they could neither fight nor flee. These animals, placed in a bag or immersed in a jar of water, died in a few minutes. The amazing fact is that they did not die from suffocation or drowning but from the slowing of breathing and heart rate until they died. This response was the opposite of the fight or flight reaction when heart rate speeds up and the animals are prepared for danger. Richter concluded that the rats had died from "hopelessness."

The key message from Justice's and Richter's books is clear: beliefs have a powerful effect on our well-being. They can defy common sense, logic, and scientific explanations if the belief is powerful enough.

It is interesting to note that most viruses and bacteria that cause human illness are normally present in our bodies. We share the environment with them constantly. Most of the time, we live in harmony with them. In fact, many of the same bacteria and viruses that cause us disease normally help to keep us well. These microorganisms are only potential disease agents, requiring other factors—such as a lowered immunity—to make them destructive to us. This helps us understand why some folks never become ill and others suffer frequent and recurrent illnesses, even though both are subjected to the same potential disease agents.

Once again, our beliefs affect us for good or ill. Beliefs can strengthen or impair our immune systems, and that's what determines whether these agents help keep us healthy or lead to illness. There is documented evidence that not only infectious disease but other life threatening illnesses, including cancer, are related to these same factors.

Is Stress the Culprit?

In recent years we've been hearing more and more about stress. Stress is touted as the cause of illness or a factor contributing to the development of illness and addictions. Yet, some people who live with enormous stress rarely become ill, addicted, or disabled. This is because it is not stress but our beliefs about stress that causes physical and emotional breakdowns. Stress, like viruses and bacteria, has the potential for causing illness; is not a direct causative agent of disease.

The good news about the power of the belief system is that we are the ones who ultimately create our beliefs, not our bodies, not our past, not our parents, not even society at large. We reinforce our beliefs every day, with every thought. And it is in our beliefs that our power lies—the power to be healthy and happy, or the power to live unhappy, unfulfilling lives. With proper beliefs, we can have that elusive, ever-desirable peace of mind.

Two Common False Beliefs

Living according to false beliefs leads to illness and addiction. The two most common false beliefs I have observed in adults are:

- I need to please others in order to be loved.

- I need to be in control of my world.

We develop these beliefs in childhood and initially they help us survive. Yet, to the degree that we learn and adopt these beliefs, we become "people pleasers" and "controllers" as adults. We can become so attached to these beliefs, clinging so tenaciously to them, and living so steadfastly by them, that we actually become "addicted" to them. In fact, we can become so addicted that we cannot stop living by them, not even long after we know that they are destroying us or causing us great pain.

Our entire life can be dedicated to pleasing others so they won't abandon us; or we can be dedicated to being in control so we won't feel vulnerable. The addiction to our beliefs can be very subtle. Many times we can deceive ourselves and think we are not "hooked" on these beliefs, when we actually are.

Chase grew up in affluence. He and his family had every advantage money could buy. His parents lived on inherited money and never had to work at a job. Scholastically, Chase never excelled. In school, he got along and always received highest grades in "conduct." His behavior was always exemplary. He had a quiet temper which seldom emerged since Chase usually got everything he wanted by "being nice."

He married Becky when he was twenty-three They met in Hawaii while on vacation and moved home to California after a whirlwind courtship and marriage in Reno. He never told his family about his marriage until he and Becky arrived at his parent's home and announced that they were husband and wife. His parents were stunned.

Chase somehow thought they would be happy for him. He could not understand their reaction, nor could they understand his. Chase and Becky got an apartment nearby and lived on an income Chase had from his grandparents—just a few hundred dollars a month—and with some part-time work they did well enough.

His personality began to change. He grew more sullen and withdrawn. Neither Chase nor his parents would compromise their views. Chase grew more depressed until I met him at the hospital after he had taken an overdose of medication prescribed for a sports injury. Beneath his depression, he was furious at his parents. He believed that being nice would change everything. He had always controlled people and events in his life by his pleasant, cooperative attitude. Now it wasn't working at all.

Even though Chase had a childhood and lifestyle different than most of ours, he learned similar lessons and had similar beliefs. He grew up believing that if he were nice to people they would be nice in return. He used niceness to control others. When it failed he become disappointed, hurt, and angry. But he could not change simply because he knew these beliefs had not worked. He was addicted to his beliefs.

This is the most common theme underlying all the problems I see in my psychiatric practice: People try to "control" others by being nice. This belief does not work because it is a "false" belief. If we are nice, other people will be nice back sometimes, but we cannot count on it. Nor can we always be in control. Having to control in order to feel okay can lead to major problems. Many major emotional breakdowns, including my own, result from years of frustration and disappointment based on trying to please others in order to be loved, or trying somehow to control the people or events in our lives.

Studies have actually demonstrated that these attempts to control other people and our environment increase the body's production of adrenalin-like hormones. These hormones eventually produce negative effects in our immune system and play a role in cardiovascular disease.

Beliefs and Symptoms

Living according to false beliefs (beliefs that are not compatible with the reality of our lives) leads to unhappiness, symptoms, or even addictions. Symptoms of anxiety, depression, panic, phobias, or obsessions are all related to living according to these false beliefs, clinging to them in an addictive way, and not being able to change them by "willing" them away.

Chase believed pleasing was enough to control people and events in his life. His earlier experience had always confirmed this. He was so "hooked" on these beliefs that he nearly died when he could not readjust them when they stopped working.

Most illnesses result from years of living according to false beliefs like Chase's. When I begin working with a client who has panic attacks, severe depression, or obsessive-compulsive symptoms I first go into the life history. It is always obvious that the disease did not begin with those symptoms. The disease began in childhood when they formed and began living by false beliefs. The symptoms of disease begin to manifest when the application of our beliefs ceases to work and we do not know how to let go of them.

Holding on to false beliefs and trying to force feed them into our lives is an even more important disease factor than genetic predisposition. We may have "biological triggers" (the term I use for this genetic predisposition), but these triggers do not have to be "pulled." We can live our lives with beliefs which do not set off symptoms.

And we can live symptom-free for the rest of our life after learning
and applying healing in our life.

What's the Answer?

New beliefs can replace old ones. Healing is a belief-changing
process.

As we shall learn in **Part II: Healing,** the first step of healing is to
identify our false beliefs, specifically the two master beliefs—pleasing others and feeling that we need to be in control.

Later in the book, we'll come to understand that spiritual surrender brings healing. Working with a Higher Power can change these
deep-seated addictive beliefs and heal us. This is a simple formula
with powerful effects.

THE FEAR OF ALONENESS

Feeling alone is so intimately connected to our feelings of self-worth that we will do anything to avoid it. We somehow overlook the fact that we always have *ourselves*. It's as if we are nobody.

One of my indelible childhood memories is a summer afternoon at a small lake in Michigan where our family—Mother, Dad and all seven of us sons were living in a rented vacation cottage. I was almost four. Dad had come home with a gift for me—a small tin boat with a rubber band driven propeller. I rushed down to the water and became engrossed in watching this tiny vessel cut a clean course from the dock to the shore (I was not allowed to go into the water alone, unsupervised). When I went back to the cottage it was empty. I ran behind the house. The family car and the family were gone. I was crushed. I stood by the road sobbing, feeling alone and abandoned.

The ending, though, was a happy one. Mother had miscounted when the family assembled in the car and thought I was aboard. At the first stop someone missed me and in a few minutes the shiny hood of Dad's black oldsmobile appeared on the horizon and the family returned to claim me.

My story is insignificant when compared to hundreds of graphic tales of cruel abandonment and desertion, often mixed with brutal abuse, that patients have endured. But it was a significant moment for me. Pain is pain. I never forgot the pain of that experience. I refelt it many times later whenever I believed I had been deserted or abandoned. The pain of that incident cost me several hundred dollars worth of tears in therapy before I ultimately became desensitized. Now, fortunately, I can laugh and feel grateful for Dad's kindness in bringing that treasured boat rather than the pain that my family's unintentional abandonment caused me.

Feeling alone or abandoned, in my experience, is one of the two experiences we seek to avoid. Many of us cannot stand to be alone without other people or activity even for an instant. Walkman radios, constant background music, blaring televisions, endless newspapers, magazines, books, other distractions, any kind of contact—these are only a few of the thousands of ways we avoid confronting the feeling of being alone. We so fear this feeling that often we watch TV and read or knit. Or we drive, chew gum, and listen to the radio! The gym where I exercise has the television and radio playing simultaneously, and most of the younger members are plugged into walkman sets as well. Triple protection! No one feels alone in our gym.

Trying to Avoid Feeling Alone and Abandoned

Sometime, early in life, we become aware of this fragile dependence on others and the fear—the deep, gut wrenching fear—of being alone began. Often my patients recount a single event, similar to mine, when the happy freedom of childhood ended and the lifelong, self-conscious fear of being alone or abandoned began. These events may be deliberately imposed on us by an abusive adult, or they can occur under the most innocent of circumstances.

Belinda was an only child. Early childhood photographs revealed a child with huge brown eyes and a shy smile. Her hands were clenched in tiny fists and she never looked directly into the camera. She had few friends, she recalled. Her mother watched her closely and seemed upset when Belinda wandered away from view—even for a few moments.

One day Belinda met another little girl in front of their apartment in Detroit and went to the other child's home and played for hours—

forgetting about everything except the fun she was having. When she returned home her mother was frantic—and furious. More furious than Belinda could remember before or since. She recalled that "something happened that day." It was as if her childhood ended.

After that she was always self-conscious and aware of what her mother—and other people—wanted. She dates the beginning of a life of "people pleasing" to that day more than forty years earlier.

Her story is not unique; on the contrary, it is common. In fact people pleasing is the most common—and frequently the most painful—belief system that I see in psychiatric practice. It seems to develop early in life, usually beginning with events like Belinda's or mine. Too often it becomes fixed in the child's mind. It becomes a compulsive or addictive way of operating in life, meaning that we no longer have a conscious choice. Choice is supplanted by a strong, continuing urge to act pleasingly. We believe that in this way we can avoid the pain of feeling rejected, deserted, abandoned, or alone. Few can stand the feelings that come with the belief that we are each alone in an uncaring universe. The irony is that we are never separate and alone in the way we believe.

People are seldom aware of how extensively this belief system affects them until they have a major breakdown, or as I prefer to call it, "breakthrough."

The panic attacks, anxiety, and depressions that I have observed are all symptoms resulting from a feeling of being alone and helpless in an uncaring universe. What is called emotional illness, in my experience, results partly from feeling totally alone and partly from feeling helpless (which is discussed in Chapter 8).

For years I was puzzled by the contradiction I noted in patients who had severe phobias or panic attacks. On the one hand they feel desperately afraid. People who experience panic attacks often believe that they will die or go insane if they are left alone, yet they are unable to trust anyone but themselves, so they are alone. I have known many patients who were afraid of driving on freeways. But when asked to describe exactly what made them fearful, it turned out that they were not afraid of having a panic attack so much as they were afraid of getting themselves into a situation where they would have to ask another person for help. ("What will people think of me?") People pleasing and fear of being out of control are at the root of their problem.

Suggestions, reassurances, and support are futile, since despite their fear of being alone they do not believe they can trust anyone. Eventually people who are able to help them, including some therapists, become frustrated and angry and refuse to continue having a relationship with them. When this happens, it of course reinforces the person's belief that they can trust no one and are all alone.

Fear, anxiety, apprehension, dread, worry, trepidation, uneasiness, awkwardness, shyness—all are connected to our feelings of aloneness and helplessness. Only by facing and accepting these feelings does healing begin to occur.

When we finally face our feelings of aloneness and accept them we discover that we are not alone. We overlook the fact that we have ourselves and our feelings—that is really having somebody, and we are really not alone. We find that there is more to us than we had considered. If this is true—and it is!—then the root of panic and anxiety can be healed.

Bartholomew, in his second book, *From the Heart of a Gentle Brother*, states:

"Fear is part of the life-cycle. When fear is with you, you can train yourself to say, 'My friend, you are here! I remember you well. You have come to tell me some part of myself needs looking at, needs explaining. I am going to sit with you, my friend, fear, until you disclose your secret to me.'

"If we will address fear as something real and helpful, rather than frustrating and terrifying, we will have finished with a great deal of the problem.

"So when we are in fear remember, anything that comes to us is our friend, whether it's nightmare or terror. If we can see it as energy approaching in order to solve a basic dilemma, we will be able to appreciate it and let the fear approach with love and caring. And something very strange happens. We begin to want to experience fear. And when we want to experience it, we know the game is almost over, because we are now ready to finish the unfinished process within ourselves. When that moment comes, things are really underway."

Inviting fear into our lives may seem like a far-fetched way to remove our fear of being alone. But I am showing that we only feel alone. We are not truly alone. Even our feelings are companions, guides, and teachers. Later when we connect with our inner child we have the excitement of experiencing a long neglected part of ourselves that created this illusion of aloneness that has caused us so much discomfort in our lives. We discover that as we acknowledge and accept our feelings we learn that we are not alone at all.

The Quest to Avoid Feeling Alone

As children, most of us are taught some version of the following: "When you are nice to others and please them, they will be nice to you." If there are universal beliefs in our society, this is surely one of them. It actually works for some people, for example, those who live in cloistered religious communities, or small agrarian communities on the fringes of civilization. Most of us get very uncomfortable when we're around compulsive people pleasers; these folks make us start looking for the nearest exit. Their desire to please can become oppressive because beneath their nice exterior there's a desire to control and manipulate us, to get us to express what a wonderful person they are.

Some people pleasers make their way into the helping professions—such as my own—where after professional training, a few fractured personal relationships, and some experience helping others to come to terms with their own people pleasing belief systems, they develop people pleasing as an art form.

I write easily about people pleasers because I am writing about myself. I don't recall being taught these beliefs but my personality and experiences convince me I learned them. A dramatic experience occurred when I was five. It's effects lingered for years, later providing me with insights about how we learn these patterns.

My brother Tom (two years younger) and I were walking to the store near our summer cottage. On the way we saw a newspaper stuffed into the end of a rural mailbox at the side of the road. Somehow we decided to take it (though I'm certain neither of us could read). I recall going to the store but having no idea what we did with the newspaper.

As we returned along the same route the owners of that cottage were standing by the road and beckoned us. I ran in panic, scream- ing until I reached home. I can still picture other neighbors watching us run by shrieking. To this day I realize I don't know if Tom was panicked or not. I told my parents we were chased, but I know they weren't convinced because nothing was done.

For years, well into high school, I was afraid to walk past that house. Whenever I would, I rushed by with sweaty palms and a rac- ing heart. My fear of confronting what I had done was so deep that I never did speak to the owners of the cottage. And for years I avoided the simple act of apologizing and facing their possible anger or resentment. I was afraid of being rejected, afraid of feeling worthless and alone.

We learn early in life to please everyone except ourselves. Some- times this is programmed by parents who were programmed by their parents and so on. We even search out people to please because it feels so good—much like being loved. The belief that pleasing will bring love and all the good things of life underlies all of what is now called codependency.

Disciples and supporters of this and other related self-effacing belief systems make up the core of the 12-Step recovery program called Codependents Anonymous. At the time of this writing, this one program may have more members in the United States than the combined membership in all our churches.

Members of Codependents Anonymous and similar groups rec- ognize and address the addictive nature of people pleasing and other doomed-to-almost-certain-failure beliefs. For many of us this and related beliefs lead to abandoning ourselves and not gaining what we need for our own nurturing. We become like reeds in the wind. We learn to neglect ourselves for the sake of others, in order to be loved by them. Many popular book titles reflect the various manifes- tations of this crippling belief system: *Do I Have To Give Up Me In Order To Be Loved By You? Women Who Love Too Much,* and *Saying Yes When You Really Mean No.*

Most of the time we are driven to please others so that they will love, admire, compliment, and respect us, think well of us, do what we want them to do and, most important of all, not abandon us. We cannot stand to feel alone. Many of us will do almost anything to avoid that terribly painful experience.

People pleasers do not know where they leave off and others begin. They are unable to establish emotional boundaries or establish reasonable limits on what they do or give to others. They have no clear idea where they stop and another person begins. They are unable to allow others to do their own thinking, worrying, suffering, and learning. In short, they find it difficult to allow others to live their own lives. When asked what they think in a group they most often look to others for the answer. When they have opportunities to speak up for themselves, they often fail because they are so accustomed to reacting to others rather than depending on themselves. They are so unfamiliar with themselves that they have no idea what they really feel.

One classic description says, "If a people pleaser were drowning, going down for the last time, someone else's life would pass before their eyes." Our own lives are so unfamiliar to us because we live them through other people.

We are the consummate givers. The only trouble is that our motives are not without selfish ends. We give in order to get—love, acclaim, recognition, support—or even just being acknowledged, so that we do not feel alone. We are dependent on others because we stake our happiness on others being pleased with us or reassuring us that we are okay. We are always looking to the outside world for confirmation that we even exist. Look at me! Notice me please! Let me do something for you so that I can feel alive and loved!

Sometimes the people pleasing belief system gets turned upside down. This often happens when, as children, people pleasers fail to get the attention they desire again and again. Then, they go in the exact opposite direction. Their way of operating becomes, "If I can't get attention by being a nice guy, maybe I can get the attention I want by doing just the opposite, by causing others a lot of grief through bad behavior." Professionals who work with juvenile delinquents often find this to be true. These young offenders frequently come from environments where it was difficult or even impossible to get positive feedback for their efforts to be helpful or loving.

"Pleasing" behaviors are often hidden efforts to control others—a goal they actually share with people users—rather than actually loving them.

People users seldom think of themselves as alone. They see others as extensions of themselves and use people much as nicotine addicts use cigarettes and alcoholics use alcohol. A standing joke in psychiatry is that people pleasers are the ones who "go crazy" while "people users" (unflatteringly called narcissists) are the ones who "drive them there."

This scenario is rarely black and white, however. Most of us have qualities of both pleasing and using other people. When I was in college I often wondered what happened when two people pleasers marry. Now I know. One of the two emerges as the pleaser while the other emerges as the user.

Many of us people pleasers (also called care takers) disguise our need to feel secure and loved behind acts of caring for others. We treat others in ways that we want to be treated, but we are afraid to ask. Or, finding someone who treats us this way, we become uncomfortable because it is an unfamiliar and awkward role for us. We continually seek out relationships where we are needed. Later, in therapy or healing, it becomes clear that this role of caring for others has become addictive. We cannot give it up or change, even after discovering how self-defeating and hurtful the pattern. Many such people enter the helping professions unknowingly, seeking satisfaction for these buried needs from helping others.

Being Alone Is Part of Being Human

Certainly there are many ways that we are alone in this world. We are alone at birth. In death we proceed alone. Learning to accept this fact, and come to terms with it, is the work of a lifetime.

When I write that we are alone, I do not mean that we have no family, friends, enemies, pets, or intestinal parasites. I mean that we do not have, own, or possess anyone but ourselves. No one can feel our pain, or joy, or face our suffering except us. No one can live or die for us. In this way we are alone.

At best we can have a sense of togetherness in our lives, a temporary perception of sharing important feelings and perceptions with others. The psychoanalyst Wilhelm Kaiser once called love and the moment of sexual orgasm the "illusion of fusion." For those brief moments we can feel like we have become a part of another person and are no longer alone. He is right. I believe it is an illusion. And always we need to be aware that these feelings of fusion are not the same as being fused.

There are a number of variations in our family backgrounds that help us understand the first step of how we got to be the way we are. These are grouped according to popular terms to describe these families. The work of John Bradshaw goes into helpful detail in describing the patterns but a few will suffice for now.

Codependent Families

These are the men and women who marry someone who needs them. They are wives and husbands of alcoholics, abusive spouses, or a host of other combinations of relationships in which one person is trying to help or please someone else. They are people "looking for love in all the wrong places."

These families are now referred to as dysfunctional (literally, "painfully functioning") families. People who grow up in these families are called codependents. This is considered by many to be a form of addiction. In the 12-Step programs designed for codependence, participants work in a healing program using the 12-Step model because they recognize that they cannot change themselves and the way they relate to others simply by "knowing" or "understanding" their patterns.

Overprotective Families

Overprotection is another disguise worn by the fear of emotional abandonment. It is yet another way that children learn to experience the feelings of being abandoned and alone. I recall one patient who taught me a lot about the hazards of overprotection.

Lee's family was enormously wealthy. When he turned thirty, his Dad, who had never held a job, insisted that Lee was lazy because he was not employed. Lee had an ideal childhood, at least from the point of view of a person who would never have to support himself. When he tried to function in the real world, he had major emotional symptoms: anxiety and panic attacks. I recall telling his parents that only "trust fund" therapy—a trust set up in Lee's name—would alleviate his symptoms. They opposed this recommendation for a while but eventually saw the wisdom of this solution and agreed. Lee was ideally suited for the life he had been raised and trained to live. Outside that restricted area he became overwhelmed.

Lee, like many others who were overprotected, had been helped into helplessness.

Perfect Families

There are no perfect families, no ideal childhoods without pain, even if that pain is the pain of not having pain. Sounds confusing, but childhoods, such as Paul and his brothers had, can be too "perfect" and not prepare them for the realities of adult living outside the family.

Paul had grown up in an "ideal" family, one that other families envied. He and his two brothers excelled at everything. They never rebelled, sat next to their mom in church, called her "Mam" and their dad "Sir." They went straight through college, married nice young women and made clear career choices. Then, shortly after he was married, Paul began waking up in the middle of the night. He suffered anxiety, a pounding heart, and fears of dying. The entire family was concerned. How could this happen to Paul? How could he have emotional problems?

They sought and received an exhaustive medical workup; all the tests came up negative. I saw Paul for evaluation and he was clearly having panic attacks. He responded to medication, yet when it was discontinued after ten weeks, his symptoms returned. The second time around he was more interested in working on the roots of his panic.

He began to see that he and his brothers were overprotected in their childhood and now ordinary life stresses precipitated panic attacks. Families like his create the illusion that we really have our family. This translates into, "I'll never have to do anything on my own." As a result, children from such backgrounds lack confidence in themselves, particularly when they have to act alone. Overprotected children become dependent and fearful adults. Paul learned his overprotective parents could do everything for him except feel his feelings. They could go everywhere with him except inside.

Paul is one of countless people I have worked with who are trained to avoid feeling alone or abandoned—and who panic when left to do something on their own. In healing they learn, as we all do, that there is someone at home inside each of us. That someone is us. We learn to love and reparent ourselves without unconditional love and caring.

Abusive Families

Disturbances in families are easy to define when one or both parents are alcoholics or emotionally ill. Their effects on the children, however, are not often recognized until many years later.

We now recognize that children growing up in these families spend much of their time and energy meeting the emotional needs and requirements of the adults. The result is predictable, unhealthy connections between the parents and children. It becomes nearly impossible to grow through the normal stages of development towards individuation and establish solid emotional boundaries.

Forced to assume adult roles as children does not eliminate the normal need to be a child, or the need to feel secure and loved. This need is merely suppressed and stays hidden and disguised throughout life.

For a child, a dysfunctional family is one in which he or she cannot devote himself or herself enough to childhood tasks, where love is lacking or, at best, given on the condition of being perfect or pleasing parents and other important people. Ideally, we'd come into life and our parents would be excited and happy about finding out who we are and figuring out ways to support us in being just who we are in the world. But, of course, this seldom occurs.

If you are from one of these homes, as most of us are, you are likely a person who tries too hard, loves too much, and seeks perfec-

tion in everything you do. Your parents probably had similar childhoods or had little in their childhoods and wanted you to have
"what they never had." A lofty goal but fraught with problems.

What's the Answer?

In our program we learn that the only place any of us can find
the comfort of unconditional love is within ourselves. We accept that
we do not have any other human beings in our lives, except ourselves, who can love us with no conditions. We are alone except for
the company of ourselves and, as we learn in healing, our own higher power or higher self. If we want to find love without conditions,
we must first give this love to ourselves. We must let ourselves in
before we can trust or love anyone else. This is why we must cease
looking for love out there and learn to love and reparent ourselves.

When I began psychiatric practice, I noticed how often the most
selfish and rejecting parents had the most dutiful and devoted children. I did not understand this. Now I do. The children were continuing their quest to get love from parents who were not able to love
them. Parents who did not receive love cannot give it. I see this constantly. Yet people almost never give up hope that they can be repar-
ented by their parents. They never give up hope that they will not
have to feel so alone.

Even when these parents are dying, their children visit them frequently, never giving up hope that they might get that one longed-
for acknowledgment of love they had never received. They ache for
an "I love you" to validate their worthiness and value. Unfortunately
they seldom hear those wonderful words, and they go on with their
lives seeking to hear those words somewhere else, addicted to the
need to be told they are loveable. Addicted to pleasing others, they
are addicted to trying to find someone, anyone, to love the love-
starved child within.

As I will describe, we find that facing our greatest fears gives us
the greatest comfort and satisfaction—finding the peace and joy that
the someone we are is identical with the God in us all.

The Peace of Aloneness

For years I have believed and taught that our aloneness is a reality that we must face; it is a source of our strength and growth. I found a meditation which says it well:

I Am At Peace With My Aloneness

There are some things I must do alone.
Breathing is not a group activity. Neither is thinking.
I acknowledge my need for relationships,
but I don't define myself totally by the
relationships that I have or by the roles I play.

I must progress in my healing by myself.
I can get the love, support, and assistance of those around me,
but the work that I need to do can't be done by the group.
It must be done by me.

At last I am aware that my growth is up to me.
Ultimately I am facing the fact of human aloneness.
This doesn't mean that I am lonely or isolated. It means that I am not resisting or denying my responsibility for my own life.
Because I recognize my autonomy and responsibility,
I am not engaged in dependent relationships
that fill an all-encompassing void.

I see myself as a whole and complete person.
I do not cling. I embrace peace with my aloneness.

DAILY AFFIRMATIONS FOR ADULT CHILDREN OF ALCOHOLICS.
HEALTH COMMUNICATIONS, 1985

THE COMPULSION TO CONTROL

Man seems desperate for control. Knowledge, possessions, recognition, perfect health, meaningful relationships. It is more than a need. It is an unhealthy addiction, one that lies at the root of all other unhealthy addictions. In fact I call our compulsive drive to be in control the Master Addiction.

Few things in life are more devastating than the feeling of powerlessness. The feeling that we are not in control of our lives is the ego's greatest fear. The ego's solution is to exert control. Control is its chief weapon against life's inevitable events. Nobody can deny that it feels wonderful when we do feel in control, be it in terms of success, wealth, fame, power, or happy relationships. All of these can provide us with feelings of well-being, though they may be fleeting. We can hardly deny that living out the dreams that our society upholds as admirable, or that our egos have built as the conditions for our happiness, fosters the sense that the more control we can exert the better things will get for us. And yet, this sense of being in control is never permanent. Something always breaks down eventually, forcing us to seek solutions outside the realm of our control.

Why does control ultimately fail us? Because the feeling of being in control is not a fact; it is an illusion. Since this feeling is never permanent it is just one more symptom of addictive thinking—substituting a false belief for reality. It is the universal symptom, yet like any drug, addictive relationship and all other symptoms of unhealthy addictions, it is satisfying only temporarily. Regardless of how impressive our show of control has been, that restless inner energy of addiction remains. It must be satisfied again and again. Feeling in control may satisfy it for a while, nothing, at least no material thing, can quiet it forever.

Our desperate need for control comes in many packages and is expressed in a variety of ways—in the quest for knowledge, or possessions, or public recognition, or in maintaining what is familiar and true. We seek it in the quest for perfect health, and for meaningful and intimate relationships.

We are willing to relinquish almost anything in life—except control. We hold on—addictively. This need to control, this fear of flux and change, even in the face of overwhelming evidence, repeated failures, continuing disappointments, is the core of all unhealthy addictions.

The need for control can wear a thousand masks. At one time it can be seen as arrogance. At another time it is disguised by being totally submissive. This need for control can be the motive behind humor, the driving force behind helping others, or the stimulus for virtually any human endeavor. As contradictory as it might seem, some people even exert control over other people by being helpless and needy. And no list would be complete without the mention of guilt, by which we seek to control other people through their fears.

The thirst for dominance can be as simple as always needing to have the last word in an argument, as complex as manipulating everyone in one's family, and as time-consuming as spending years searching for "the answer," as I have done. It can be as rudimentary as avoiding cracks in the sidewalk, or as intricate as rituals for checking and rechecking every door, window, appliance, bottle, or glass for fear that it harbors danger.

Control is spawned from fear. No matter how it is labeled, it lies at the heart of all conflict, fueling the battle of the sexes, breeding marital discord, parent-child clashes, motivating adventurers in their conquests and generals in their wars. Control underlies the need for mastery, power, domination. More than any other factor, control energizes unhealthy addictions. It is the most universal human effort to shun fear, the fear of emptiness—the inner void.

The need for control and the addictive quest for dominance is a universal quest aimed at avoiding the inner void. Because of its scope, and because it forms the underpinnings of all unhealthy addictions, it has won itself the label as the Master Addiction.

Control has many labels. Bullheaded, obstinate, mulish, inflexible, resolute, stubborn, and strong-willed are all synonyms of control. Some are euphemisms like dedicated, persevering, tenacious, persistent, or perfectionistic. All express reluctance to relinquish control. Many of these, in moderation, are healthy, allowing us to achieve worthy goals. All are intended to help us maintain command and to avoid feeling emptiness—the void. It is not *being* in control that is unhealthy; rather, it is *having* to be in control.

Symptoms of Control

Fear and the desire to retaliate are the most common symptoms of our need for control. It can be helpful to think of these as "fear" and "attack."

Fear is usually the first symptom when control is threatened. Fear precedes anger, but the transition is so rapid that often we are not aware of the fear, just the anger.

Attack, the impulse to retaliate either by thoughts, words or actions, is a response to fear. Attack is the response to feeling powerless. It is the ego's way of defense. Loss of control is so painful and so unfamiliar that we take action. We take the offensive. We attack.

Kathy was obsessed with a fear that she was going to harm someone in her family. She had stopped cooking because she was afraid she might poison the food using contaminated ingredients or put medication, rat poison, Draino or some other deadly concoction in their food.

These "crazy" ideas contrasted with her appearance. She was an attractive, neatly groomed forty-seven-year-old mother of three sons with a responsible job at a university which she very much enjoyed. Her piercing brown eyes had a humorous twinkle which seemed to belie her painful obsession. At work she was only bothered occasionally when she went into a storeroom where chemicals were kept. She seemed to live in two worlds. A world of fear and obsession at home and one of near-peace at work.

Her husband Rico had always been the one concerned about food. For years he insisted on checking everything she cooked "to see if it was fresh." Numerous times he had doubts and dialed the Poison Hotline inquiring about 'certain foods she was preparing. Her breakdown, though, occurred around a single incident.

Hurrying home from a basketball game she suggested to Rico that they buy fast food for the family. She was tired and didn't feel like cooking. Rico protested and reminded her of some hamburger in the freezer that she could defrost and cook. Reluctantly she agreed. She dragged herself through the process of preparing the meal. When she sat down, the others had already finished eating. The hamburger tasted "bad" to her. Kathy panicked, called the Poison Hotline and her family physician. In the interim she had Rico and her three boys vomit their dinner. Her physician concluded that the odor from other food in the freezer may have gotten into the hamburger. He added that even if the meat had been bad, slight diarrhea would have been the most likely result, not the paralysis or death that she feared.

From that day on her fears spread. She could not go into the kitchen to cook or even be around food while it was being prepared.

Kathy's story demonstrates two points. First, it illustrates how fear can be contagious, like the flu. Her husband Rico was fearful, and gradually his fear affected her. On the other hand, his constant harassment in the kitchen irritated her and undermined her self-confidence. Eventually his "attacks" led to her retaliation. His obsession became her obsession, though in a disguised way. Kathy took Rico's fears and developed an obsession whereby she "outfeared the fearful one."

By the time they consulted me, three years had passed. Rico was angry because he had been forced to take on responsibility for all the cooking. Kathy was caught up in her fears which disguised her anger and her attack feelings toward Rico. She had gained "crazy" control through the obvious power struggle in their relationship.

Competition

Competition is another symptom of control, also based on fear. Competition can be a healthy symptom and contribute to a balanced life. But however you look at it, competition is still a symptom of control. It implies a winner and a loser. Winning can help us feel self-confident, enhance social relationships, and provide many happy hours for participants and viewers alike. Losing can be healthy or destructive, depending on whether or not we view losing as intrinsic to our worth. Winners are not better than losers, except in that competition. Wherever we encounter the need to win or the drive to compete, we are looking at symptoms of control.

Many people seek to avoid feeling alone or powerless through competition, through having better wives, wealthier husbands, brighter kids, flashier cars, sexier bodies, more expensive homes, more exotic vacations, or larger net worth. Alas, how we struggle to avoid feeling, facing, and accepting that we do not truly possess any of these. Competition provides nothing more than a temporary "fix," the shaky illusion of being better, brighter, or somehow of more value than others. Because a part of us always knows that the illusion is shaky, we live in fear. We know that at any moment the illusion can be shattered.

Understanding

Understanding or explaining the human experience is another one of the ways that we attempt to control our lives. Insights, as we call them in psychiatry, are like little "fixes," small doses of mind-drugs that calm our fears for a little while. But understanding and insight are symptoms of our need for control. Like our other ways of control, the need to understand, when it is out of balance, can itself become an unhealthy addiction.

The need to know, to understand, is the cornerstone of analytical psychiatry. The traditional theory of psychoanalysis holds that we can liberate ourselves from fear and conflict through understanding the unconscious motives behind them. This has not proven to be true in practice, however. For years I challenged other psychiatrists who supported this belief. It was not until rather late in my life, after I had accepted my own addictive need for control, that I recognized what really happens, how this form of psychiatry reinforces the addiction to control and is a "drug" in itself.

There is a major difference between traditional psychiatry and healing with a spiritual base. In psychiatry we not only use insights to help our patients regain control; we use medication as well. We are trained to help our patients be in control, not to surrender control. But surrendering control validates our own experiences in 12-Step recovery programs or other spiritual programs like A Course In Miracles.

This is not to say that insight has no purpose in recovery. It is a valuable tool, but again it is not the whole answer. Understanding and insight can provide us with road maps, locating where we might go to get in touch with who we are, but no matter how well-illustrated these maps may be, they are not the journey itself.

Pleasing Others

Pleasing other people is the most subtle symptom of control—and often the most difficult to recognize. Caring and concern for others' welfare and the desire to help are wonderful human characteristics. There is one essential quality, however, that distinguishes a Mother Teresa from a Wicked Witch of the West. That quality is found in asking why we are being pleasing, helpful and nice. What are the conditions attached to our care and compassion?

In psychotherapy the most constant challenge is to help people "come off it," to assist them in owning up to their "real motives" for helping others. It is difficult for any of us to believe that our motives for doing nice things for others might not be so nice after all. One example particularly comes to mind, occurring during an Al-Anon meeting I was attending in 1986:

Sonia, a young woman, the unhappy second wife of a physician, was leading the discussion and relating her struggles in her relationship. Her husband was twenty years older than she, had grown children of his own, and was more concerned about his health and plans for retirement than with their three-year-old daughter. At first I barely listened. But she began talking about her discovery that her "people pleasing," a quality her husband loved and admired, "was not nice at all." She related her discovery of her rage when her people pleasing did not impact him in the direction she wanted. Her voice rose. I paid closer attention. She had seemed so genuinely "nice" at meetings before. I had felt attracted to her for that reason.

She became sarcastic, belittling her husband's fears about his health and retirement, yet aware what she was doing. Her rage was clearly evident. No sign of people pleasing remained. I didn't reflect on Sonia for long. I began thinking about myself.

At that moment I saw, really saw, that my lifelong pattern of relating to my world was like Sonia's. People pleasing was one of the masks worn by my need to control. When it failed to achieve the results I desired I felt similar rage, or at least became irritated. How long had I denied that! How long my ego had protected me until my life was in such chaos that these meetings felt life-saving.

Only when we completely surrender, giving up every condition that we might attach to the help we offer others, do we become truly helpful. Only when we surrender the illusion that we know the path that others should follow to get well, or to improve their lives can our help be beneficial. To insist upon compliance to our own wishes is one of the greatest blocks to establishing a healing relationship. Until we surrender control in this area our compassion and care are nothing more than the masks of another addiction.

Denial

Denial is the most familiar pretense of control. Denial is a way of masking our pain and weaving an illusion that we are in control by disavowing any connection between our symptoms and ourselves. Denial says "if I don't acknowledge or admit it, it does not exist." Denial is an unconscious process, one that blocks the first step toward healing, the ability to say, "I have a problem. I am the problem." Or as Pogo puts it, "We have found the enemy and the enemy is us."

Denial is very evident in my psychiatric practice. Some patients, for example substance abusers, frequently claim, "I can quit any time I want to!" The falseness of this claim is nearly always obvious to everyone except the person saying it. Yet substance abusers are not the only ones who exercise denial. Patients with anxiety and depression will deny their need to control the parts of their life that are beyond their control, while their symptoms continue to be a testimony to that fact.

The power of denial strikes me every time I walk into my office. Several filing cabinets filled with charts of past patients attest to the fact that much of my work as a psychiatrist involves patients who want nothing more than the alleviation of their pain so that they can resume their denial. So many seek immediate relief, a "fix." Those who move on, who finally go out of denial and discover the willingness to look into themselves, usually do so after all else has failed and the pain of changing becomes less than the pain of continuing as they are.

Projection

Projection is another symptom of our need to control, closely related to denial. The way this works is fascinating. We maintain our illusion of control by denying our own feelings or motives and projecting them onto other people. This process has been compared to a movie theater—only this time the film is inside our heads and the screen upon which we're projecting is other people and the world around us. We of course don't see ourselves doing this. We can be quite convinced that what we perceive is true because we find "evidence" for our illusions in other people. We react to our denied feelings and attitudes as if they originated in the other person. Projection is the most common yet trickiest symptom of control.

A common example of projection is seeing another person as unfriendly and then using that perception to "justify" our own unfriendliness. This results from feeling afraid of that person and "projecting" our fear onto them. Sometimes our projections draw the unfriendly people to us. Sometimes our own projections distort friendly people into unfriendly ones. But in every case, we look at our projections and say, "You see, this is proof that I have to feel as I do. This justifies my own feelings of unfriendliness and anger." As long as we cling to our belief in our projections we don't have to look at the real source of our feelings—ourselves.

Projection can be a very transient thing. How much better the world seems to us on the days we feel happy. How much worse the world seems on days we feel afraid.

We are constantly projecting the results of past experiences into present situations. Everything is colored by us. One of the best ways to refocus on attention, and to take a look at the real source of our feelings, is to go back to the image of the movie theater any time we find ourselves blaming others for our fear or irritation. Look upon what's happening at that moment as if you are a movie projector with the film continually running inside your head. Every experience you have is your own movie, projected onto the screen of a person or object or situation outside you.

For years I was puzzled over why I was more comfortable with women than men. As I uncovered my own projections I realized I "projected" my own fears and competitiveness toward men; I saw them as trying to dominate and control me. With women I projected a desire for them to like me, something I always sought from my mother. I projected what I feared onto other men, and projected what I wanted on to women. Both projections were based on my own unconscious inner movie, which had nothing to do with the other people involved. In both instances, the projections were my own unwitting attempt to feel in control in my relationships.

The Struggle to Give Up Control

When I think of control, I always recall Julian. How many times I sat with him over the years we worked together, trying to help him calm his raging fears and panic. His breakdown began with an infestation of pubic lice (the "crabs") contracted in a Tiajuana jail cell (where he was jailed for refusing to pay for an unsolicited photograph of himself with a near-naked lady at a bar). An apparently "paid-off" policeman hustled him off in handcuffs when he cursed the photographer. From this simple and easily treated condition, contracted in the unsanitary jail cell, Julian developed a complex series of fears and rituals which took years to calm and unravel.

Julian was the youngest of three sons from a close family. He had never had a similar experience. The repercussions of his first trip to

Mexico and his first drunk resulted in feelings never before encountered. He felt completely powerless and out of control as a result of both the parasites and his night in jail. Long after the "little critters" were shampooed away he imagined them crawling on his body. He stopped sleeping, washed his clothes over and over again, and began to fear germs and illness. He feared touching anyone, using any bathroom but his own. He washed himself for hours and avoided most public places for fear that he be contaminated.

He was barely able to teach his classes at a local college. He needed to time his trips to the bathroom so he would never have to use the facilities at school, even the bathroom in his private office. I found it hard to visualize that this tall, handsome young man with piercing gray eyes and a ready smile could be crippled by fears. When he wasn't petrified by phobias he had a wonderful sense of humor. I liked him immediately. Yet, no amount of reassurance from me (or anyone) could free him of his obsession about germs and illness.

Julian's story offers a dramatic example of how powerful control, and the need to feel in control can be. Julian had lived a protected life, probably overprotected. When he was confronted with the parasites and a night in jail, he felt overwhelmed and out of control. He panicked and the panic spread until he became nearly crippled as he drastically changed his life in a futile effort to regain his illusion of control. His control had been breached and he became obsessed with preventing a recurrence. There is more, much more, to Julian's story but his initial breakdown is a dramatic example of how central control can be in maintaining our sense of well-being.

Other emotional illnesses parallel Julian's. Panic attacks, with uncontrollable fear, rapid heart rate and shortness of breath, for an example, result when emotional control is threatened. The fear of heart attacks, dying, or going insane that panic patients experience are all imagined outcomes of a loss of control. The need to be in control is so powerful in patients who panic that their recoveries are often lengthy. This need for control far exceeds their capacity to trust others. They are frightened, alone, and trapped in their own fears.

Only trust, surrendering to the fearful feelings, can help people like Julian to erase their pain. Depression, especially major depression, is also intimately bound to loss of control. As you recall, my own breakdown occurred suddenly, though after many months of stress. I felt as if I'd been a punctured balloon with all the air let out of me. Looking back, there was little reality in my fear. There was no threat to my life. I was hardly on the verge of bankruptcy. Despite that, I broke down. I could not surrender. I was unable to let go and trust that the outcome could possibly be favorable.

Substance abuse, cigarette smoking, eating disorders, compulsive gambling or shopping, and addictive relationships of all kinds, all result from attempts to maintain or remain in control. Eventually these unhealthy addictions fail us, and breakdowns occur—small ones or large ones. All breakdowns and addictive symptoms result from trying to control the uncontrollable, refusing to surrender, and being unable to trust.

Facing the Master Addiction

The compulsive need for control is our most deep-seated and powerful addiction. It is lodged in our beliefs, coloring all our activities, particularly our thinking. It is our ego's most potent weapon. The belief that we must be in control forms the groundwork for all unhealthy addictions. That is why we call it the master addiction.

The desire for control often seems to emerge from our lack of it during childhood. During those years when we are acutely aware of our dependence on others for our survival and support, we experience our powerlessness. From that is born our fears. Our entire society, including psychiatry, is geared toward supporting the belief that we can quell our fears by gaining control over physical illness, emotional dysfunction, substance abuse, or other disruptions of our lives.

Healing involves the opposite of control. It comes to us by surrendering to someone or something we trust. Although we surrender control, this does not mean that we must resign from the human race or give into every demand, allowing ourselves to be exploited or manipulated. What is most important is that we give over control to someone who is trustworthy. For me, it was the spiritual energy I discovered in myself, the God of my understanding.

The surrender involved in this process is perfectly expressed in the Serenity Prayer heard so often in 12-Step meetings:

God, grant me the serenity
to accept the things I cannot change,
the courage to change the things I can,
and the wisdom to know the difference.

When We Are Ready for Healing

With this chapter we conclude Part I, **The Breakdown Process.** While it can be difficult to look at the roots of our addictions, and the many behaviors and beliefs we have held on to in our effort to feel in control of our lives, that recognition opens the door to a truly new way of life.

The healing path we will now explore together is aimed at getting to the core of our pain and finally being able to choose happiness.

PART

2

The
Healing
Process

STEPS TO HEALING

Emotional breakdowns are the beginning of hope, not the end.

One morning, more than a year after my breakdown, I awoke without the slightest fear or depression. This occurred exactly three weeks after I increased the dosage of antidepressant medication to the highest level I could tolerate without being disabled by side-effects. It was Saturday and I, my mother, and my three surviving brothers were gathering in Phoenix to celebrate mother's eighty-fifth birthday. Mom had overcome her fear of flying, bolstered by a heavenly barrage of rosaries, and had come west from Kalamazoo on the pretense (constructed by her sons) that she was attending a medical convention focused on the health of senior citizens. How mother enjoyed that weekend! Adding to her delight was that fact that she would have her sons to herself, since wives had not been included in this celebration. It was monumental for me too. It was the day I began to believe I would get well.

Healing, I believe, begins the moment we stop trying to exert control over our emotions and start getting closer to them. When denial dies, recovery begins. It does not matter if surrender is voluntary or, like mine and millions who have emotional breakdowns, mandated by our collapse. At the precise moment when we are convinced that things couldn't be worse, that's the dawn of recovery. At that moment when we reach out to get help from some one or some thing, that's when we have taken the first step of our healing. The attitude of "I can care for myself" collapses and becomes, "I must have help or I'm not going to make it!" Alcoholics and other substance abusers call this bottoming out. When our emotions overwhelm us, making it impossible to continue functioning in our usual way, that's called breakdown.

Emotional breakdowns are often the only way many of us can say "No, this is enough!," or "I don't want to." At the time it occurs it is the only way we know to stake out our emotional boundaries, release our trapped feelings, or give up control. Breakdowns let us take a break from a life which is no longer tolerable and to momentarily release ourselves from addictive patterns in our lives. They protect us from the further onslaught of difficult relationships or from a way of life that has been strangling us.

Breakdowns take endless forms, ranging from violent outbursts erupting from a lifetime of buried frustration to quiet withdrawal, resulting from exhaustion and the inability to handle one more assault from life. There are a number of common patterns with similar if not identical symptoms, since emotional upsets all stem from fear. The masks of emotional collapse range from a single, annoying symptom to total loss of the ability to function.

When my breakdown came so suddenly and unexpectedly that November morning in 1981, I could hardly have believed that it would be the beginning of my recovery from a lifetime of addiction to control. But it was. The pain penetrated deep into my core being, crushing every defense I had built against the loss of control. It touched every part of my personal history, from my days as a scared, skinny, blue-eyed kid in Kalamazoo, through each experience in high school, college, medical school, and my life as a psychiatrist. Several years would pass before I fully appreciated what had happened to me that day: Help had finally arrived!

Finally, when I had no choice, I surrendered to the power of my buried feelings. My final defense, my pride, had crumbled, and I began to find the help I needed.

As I think about that turning point in my life, two important sayings echo in my mind. They are: "The teacher will appear when the student is ready," and "Healing begins the moment that control over our emotions ends."

The Source of Healing Is Within Us

Healing involves a new way of perceiving ourselves—from within. Pain generated by breakdowns forces us to look inside for our answers. This begins with recognizing and trusting our feelings, first expressed as the symptoms of our breakdowns. We then follow these feelings to the beliefs from which they originate. Change comes as we change the beliefs, which we often find to be based on incomplete or inaccurate information that we had as children.

When anxiety and depression crippled me, I no longer thought of anything outside myself. Pain seized and held my attention. Whenever it left, I was absorbed in the anticipation of when it would return. Jim, an electronic technician with whom I worked many years later, clearly described the kind of pain that most people experience with a breakdown when he said, "I never was properly introduced to pain until I met this pain."

When we are in the middle of a breakdown, we cease blaming, analyzing, or searching out there for answers. We no longer look for scapegoats or insights. We only want RELIEF. Everything else seems meaningless—relationships, psychological formulas, religion or spirituality. All seem shallow in the face of such pain.

I recall reading passages in spiritual books at night during my breakdown (the pain of depression is often much less at night), and finding some comfort in them. In the morning, however, when the pain returned, the same words meant nothing.

Nothing outside ourselves heals us, I learned. We heal from within. Medication can certainly help but it cannot heal our wounds. Close relationships can aid enormously but they cannot cure us. Recovery groups can be wonderfully supportive but they do not heal. Prayers do not heal us either. We heal with guidance and help from all of these; medication (when indicated), therapists, recovery groups, prayers *and* a belief-changing spiritual program. I have heard of other ways of healing, including what is called Rational Recovery programs, but my experience makes me skeptical of their claims.

The major role of help is to provide a safe atmosphere where we can take down the barriers that we have erected against our own healing.

The Elements of This Program

A true healing journey treats the whole person: body, mind/emotions, and spirit. Though we are not divided into parts, we rely on symbols or metaphors (ego, inner child, etc.) to discuss treatment of each of these areas of our lives.

This program separates healing into three major areas.

1. **Restoration**—Stabilizing the body and emotions

2. **Reparenting ourselves**—Releasing buried emotions

3. **Reprogramming**—Recognizing and changing addictive beliefs

Restoration

When we see people in pain, we must first find the pain; take out the thorn and then treat the wound.

When dealing with emotional breakdown, the first order of business is to quiet the pain. Restoration is the reestablishment of emotional and physical equilibrium.

Severe emotional pain causes biochemical changes in the brain and body. Often the quickest and best means to begin the healing process is medication. Then, once equilibrium is restored, we can focus our attention on the cause of our pain.

Reparenting Ourselves

Reparenting ourselves is a process of reconnecting with denied, buried, unfelt feelings from earlier in life, beliefs that motivate the behaviors which lead to our breakdowns.

Feelings from childhood, particularly those forbidden by families and others, are buried alive within us. Even though they are buried, their energy continues to affect us. Fear of experiencing these feelings (e.g., fear of losing control or being abandoned) continues to imprison us in familiar patterns of behavior. Caught up in these patterns, it can seem to us that we are powerless, that we can't change, except temporarily.

Reparenting ourselves consists of providing an inner atmosphere of safety and trust for ourselves, one where we can feel all the buried, frightening, forbidden unfelt feelings. We become our own parents, the parents we wish we had during our childhood, parents our parents did not know how to be.

We achieve this by learning to love all of our feelings, and by feeling our feelings without criticizing, judging, or restricting them. In the reparenting process, whatever we feel is okay.

A trained therapist, skilled in helping us connect with these feelings or emotions, can help tremendously. In order to forgive and forget painful memories it is first important to feel them, drain their energy and redirect that energy into our healing. We need to feel hurt, anger, loneliness, helplessness, all the feelings of the emotionally wounded, abused, or abandoned child within us. We feel to heal.

Reprogramming Beliefs

We reprogram our beliefs, recognizing and changing the beliefs that underlie our unhealthy addictions. We use principles found in structured programs that have proven successful in overcoming unhealthy addictions. The major areas of reprogramming involve the struggle between our Master Addiction and our need to feel in control and programs that teach us to trust and relinquish or surrender control.

In our program we use the principles in the so-called 12-Steps, originally drafted by founding members of Alcoholics Anonymous. The beliefs in these principles reach the core of fear and distrust which underlie unhealthy addictions. They guide us to heal the wounds that cripple us by yielding to an inner or higher source of healing than our own ego. The 12-Steps offer a form of cognitive therapy, a belief changing, spiritual program which guides each person step-by-step from an emotional breakdown to recovery and healing.

Other spiritual programs which use similar principles are also valuable. Many religious organizations using principles found in the Bible offer the same belief-changing principles. One must be cautious in finding religious teachers however, much like one must be cautious in seeking psychiatrists. Avoid ones who use the Bible as a device to reinforce fears by teaching of a punishing or vindictive God in the place of a God who loves us unconditionally despite our unhealthy addictions.

A Course In Miracles (see Chapter 12 for a fuller description of both of these programs) is another excellent spiritual program which offers a complete course in healing our unhealthy addictive beliefs. After many years of searching, I have chosen this program as the one to use along with the 12-Steps.

Resistance to Spirituality

Spirituality, as taught and practiced in this program, I describe in this book is not a religion. Religion implies theology (a structured set of beliefs about God), an institution (with clergy and dogmas), buildings, and rituals. Many of us from so-called "religious" backgrounds were force-fed the institutional form of religion as children. We associate spirituality with that experience and dismiss spiritual programs such as the 12-Steps or A Course In Miracles without investigating them. Religious people may be spiritual, and spiritual people may or may not have religious affiliations. The two may or may not coexist.

Spirituality in its simplest form is anything non-material. Anything which cannot be defined by our senses (touch, taste, smell, hearing, or vision) is spiritual. For example, human consciousness cannot be detected with the senses, quantified or seen. It is a spiritual concept.

To succeed in this healing journey, we don't have to believe in God (meaning someone who pulls our strings). Recovery asks for a willingness to acknowledge some power other than ourselves (the one who messed us up), whether that power is Jesus Christ, Jehovah, Buddha, Nature, Mighty Mouse, or a nameless personal belief that there is a higher power that guides us. The main point is that we recover with the help of a power or concept of truth other than our own ego.

Why a Combined Approach

Medication alone cannot heal.

Medication can only reduce or alleviate symptoms, making it possible for us to become comfortable enough to look further for answers. Its effects prepare us for further stages of healing, reparenting ourselves, and changing addictive beliefs. Medication by itself doesn't change beliefs and thus cannot heal us. Sixty to ninety percent of the patients who are treated with medication only have relapses—often in a few weeks or months. Medications can restore imbalances in neurotransmitters (the chemical messengers of the brain and nervous system). What medications do, they do well, but they are not the answer.

Psychotherapy alone cannot heal.

Psychotherapy, particularly methods relying on understanding the connections between childhood experiences and present symptoms, are seldom effective in restoring changes in neurotransmitters seen in emotional addictions. Understanding (or insight as it is called) functions, I believe, similar to a mild tranquilizer. It calms fears but is seldom powerful or long-lasting enough to alleviate the deep-seated roots of addiction. We have seen that addictive beliefs are learned in childhood, that the disorders they manifest are chronic and deeply rooted. Changing thoughts and beliefs alone offers a long-term solution. Some forms of psychotherapy (Rational Emotive Therapy, Cognitive Therapy are examples) do change beliefs. They do not recognize these beliefs as addictions and do not encourage continuing reinforcement of new, healthier beliefs to insure continuing healing.

12-Step or other spiritual programs alone cannot heal.

12-Step programs, and other spiritual programs, can overlook or undertreat addictive beliefs that are at the root of emotional breakdowns, panic disorder, major depression or anxiety. Failing to treat the underlying beliefs would be similar to treating an alcoholic or drug addict without requiring them to stop using drugs. Until we recognize emotional disorders as addictions, they remain inadequately treated.

In my experience, failure to provide reparenting experiences for patients with buried pain from childhood blocks recovery more than any other omission. Substitute addictions develop when only one expression of the addictive energy is addressed, because hidden feelings only manifest as another addiction. I have seen this frequently at 12-Step meetings where members report attendance at several different 12-Step groups simultaneously—attending one group for alcohol abuse, another for cocaine, another for codependence, etc. Their addictions move sideways, and the addictive energy that has its source in dysfunctional beliefs continue to be expressed in unhealthy ways.

Summary

Emotional addictions are chronic disorders eventually producing symptoms that result from beliefs that we have learned in childhood. Once these chronic symptoms are adequately treated through a combined program of medication (when indicated), uncovering and desensitizing buried feelings, and addressing the beliefs underlying emotional addictions, our healing journeys can successfully continue. As the journey progresses, it has been my experience—both personally and with my clients—that we begin to recognize spiritual values and their importance in our lives. I believe that our opening up to this aspect of our lives is the natural outcome of following a program like the one described here.

In this chapter, we've explored the basic principles of healing and some of the basic modalities of treatment. We will now take each step of the program and explore it in some detail. We begin with the first part of the three-step program—restoring physical balance.

RESTORING PHYSICAL BALANCE

The skillful use of medication,
when necessary, is a life-saving gift.

It is nearly impossible to describe emotional pain. Those of us who have recovered constitute a silent fellowship, formed during the endless hours each of us has suffered alone, learning from that pain, eventually emerging into the light as we learned pain's message and it finally receded. We know what our brothers and sisters feel during those times. That pain is our dues for lifelong membership in this fellowship. Forever after, a simple knowing glance is all each of us requires to convey our bond and express our compassion for each other. Lasting friendships can begin in that instant of recognition, much like war buddies bond for life.

During my breakdown I no longer debated anything—who was to blame, what day it was, whether or not I needed medication. I did not concern myself with whether or not I was becoming addicted to drugs. Medication, I believed, made it possible to continue living, and that's about all that interested me.

Symptoms vary widely, ranging from panic and anxiety to depression and phobias. Relationships are disturbed. Jobs and marriages are jeopardized. Many fear they are "going crazy." It is futile to mention addictive beliefs or discuss spiritual healing with anyone in such severe pain. The first order of business is quieting pain, most often with medication.

I call this period of reestablishing emotional and physical equilibrium Restoration.

Factors Affecting Addictions

Growing up in troubled families is like living in a war zone, sometimes worse. When family members agree to deny the existence of problems, a kind of inner "split" occurs. Children operate as if there are no problems, yet their bodies react to the fearful reality around them, constantly pumping adrenalin. There is seldom peace. When there is, it is temporary. Daily living is a constant emotional drain. Brain researchers tell us that such continuous emotional stress wreaks gradual havoc on body and brain chemistry. Family members are continually vigilant, always tense, defensive, and prepared to protect themselves from threat or danger. The effect is a gradual wearing away, not only of psychological security, but physiological defenses as well. Surprisingly many do not break down until much later in their lives, when they have grown well into adulthood. Some survive without breakdowns. There are clearly differences in individual predispositions and responses to the unpredictable uproar and chaos of dysfunction.

Adult emotional disorders begin with dysfunctional childhoods. These disorders are chronic illnesses long before symptoms become apparent or are diagnosed. They are often triggered, but not caused by, the events we attribute to them, such as job changes, recent divorce, financial losses, moving across the country, or failing to pass an important examination. Stress factors, generally considered the cause of emotional symptoms, are in fact merely like a sudden power surge that blows the circuits.

Genetic and biological factors operate as well. Emotional disorders frequently run in families. Though some family members are spared, others suffer recurrent bouts of mania, depression, panic, or major problems in relationships, when exposed to the same apparent stressors. Patterns of poor communication, alcoholism, violation of personal boundaries, lack of respect for "emotional space," as well as general unhappiness abound in families whose members suffer these conditions. Genetic factors are often difficult to separate from environmental ones. Despite differing causes there is always reason for hope and the healing journeys are virtually the same.

Stressful events merely expose the tip of an iceberg. Deep roots of fear reach far beneath the surface. Many times emotional disorders are predated or masked by symptoms of alcoholism, drug abuse, or other addictive behaviors.

The suffering from these conditions is much more than "a case of nerves," as physicians often tell patients. Ask anyone with severe emotional symptoms. They will tell you these fear-based conditions grow beyond an illness. Fear becomes a way of life. Emotional illness is only one way of packaging fear.

From my experience, psychotherapy, counseling, or 12-Step and other spiritual programs are not powerful enough by themselves to restore the biological balance disrupted by years of stress. Our brains produce a limited amount of the adrenalin-like hormones necessary to maintain emotional balance. Breakdowns result. These breakdowns can be so subtle that the patient believes what he or she feels is "just me." Believing in the value of medication allows for its proper use during this Restoration phase of the healing journey.

When Medication Is Indicated

Whenever a patient's daily functioning is impaired to the degree that he or she cannot concentrate on ordinary activities; when they seem to be "going under"; or when their emotional circuits seem to be clearly overloaded, I consider medication.

If the person's sleep, diet, social patterns, work habits, or any other activity is disrupted, there's an excellent chance to suspect that they are overloaded. Many times the overload can seem "normal" to us because we have lived most of our life that way. We're not even aware that what we're feeling could be any different. Only objective evaluation and testing can help such people realize that not everyone feels tired all the time, collapses in front of the television nightly, sleeps all weekend, or does not have the patience or concentration to read the daily newspaper. A trial on medication may be helpful when there is doubt, allowing them to have the experience of living their life without the high level of stress they have come to associate with "normal" living.

The medications now available are safer and have fewer side-effects than earlier ones. Often in my practice, I have seen how a "trial" period on medication can be transforming. Symptoms which are thought to be part of another illness, or simply an integral part of one's personality, can be relieved. Sometimes, behavior patterns shift dramatically as the person discovers them to be caused by hidden and unrecognized emotional disorders. There's one example, in particular, that comes to mind at this moment:

"I don't know what good a psychiatrist will do. My only problem is pain," she said, as she hobbled into my office.

Shelly was forty-three, ten years divorced, with two married daughters. She lived alone, supported herself as a computer specialist, and lived in virtual isolation because of constant pain in her lower back and throughout both legs. She was seeing an orthopedist who specialized in chronic pain, a psychotherapist, and a neurosurgeon. She was undergoing physical therapy twice a week and had been taking a small dose of a minor tranquilizer for over a year. Her main concern was that I would "take it away." Since I was the first psychiatrist she had ever met she was wary.

She was a pretty, petite, youngish-looking woman who smiled brightly, despite her obvious pain. Her wide-eyed expression was one that I might have seen in the face of a person just coming out of a horror movie. She sat upright, poised on the edge of the chair as if she were a missile ready for launching. Shelly was clearly knowledgeable about her disease, diagnosed as myofascitis. She said that before she became crippled, three years earlier, she had been a compulsive exerciser, and had even taught aerobics classes. Now her life was limited to work and sitting or lying down at home. She felt hopeless and said so.

After referral to our biofeedback therapist she was only slightly less tense. She still felt hopeless.

She admitted feeling continually depressed. Her life consisted of painfully dragging herself to work or to her doctors, then collapsing at home. When I asked if she'd ever considered suicide, her smile faded, and she tearfully described her plan. She had been carefully stockpiling tranquilizers, waiting until she had enough to be certain she would be successful. She dated her depression back to childhood. She agreed to a trial of antidepressants, though without enthusiasm.

Three weeks later she burst into my office. Her report was impressive. She had begun to feel better two days after beginning medication, on a very low dosage. When she increased her dose on my recommendation severe side effects forced her back to the lower amount. Though she still had pain, she told me "my depression is a hundred times worse than the pain." Her healing journey had clearly begun.

Few patients respond as quickly as Shelly, but her story is similar to others I see, many of whom suffer from chronic emotional disorders, masked by physical illnesses or substance abuse. Remember that Shelly had two years of psychotherapy, nearly three years of pain management, and her condition had not improved. Yet, after only a few days on antidepressants she began to feel restored, sparking the beginning of her transformation.

Is this really a frequent occurrence? Yes, it is. Why? I think it is because most people still look upon emotional disorders as weaknesses. Added to this, medication is thought of as just another sign of this weakness, another dependency, and therefore more proof that they are not strong enough to overcome their problem. I am amazed at how many people I meet who still think of taking pills as lack of will power, poor motivation, or a character flaw. They may be so convinced that emotional disorders are weaknesses that they simply deny the problems they're having. For people who have at least appeared to function well in their lives—like Shelly—despite clinical problems, and despite pain that pushes them to seriously consider suicide, medical treatment of emotional disorders or the emotional component of physical disorders are too often overlooked, sometimes with tragic results.

Though the evidence is overwhelming that emotional chaos causes major physiological disruptions, many patients are still subjected to psychotherapy, particularly behavioral and cognitive therapy, which are woefully inadequate for the initial treatment of disturbances such as Shelly's.

Chad was referred to me after hearing that I had been through a major depression myself. He was in his mid-fifties, smallish, with deep-set eyes that looked dull and sad at the same time. He watched me carefully through the initial interview, seeming to be looking for something in me that would help him immediately. He had experienced extreme fatigue for eighteen months and had fought seeking help. The treatments he had selected were designed to treat his symptoms as if he had a relatively simple physical disorder. When I saw him he was undergoing acupressure, two forms of massage, and chiropractic treatments. He had tried a host of therapies earlier. None had brought anything but temporary relief.

Only recently had he seen a psychiatrist for the first time and was taking a low dose of an antidepressant medication, too low since it had not begun to alleviate the depression. His feelings of hopelessness and despair filled my office.

He was suicidal and barely able to teach his classes at the university. He read me a suicide note he had written to his wife during our first visit. I was touched by the passion I sensed buried beneath his pain. I found myself choking back my own tears as I empathized with this person who mirrored what I had been feeling just a few years earlier. I was convinced that his suicidal intentions were real.

The first task was clear. Chad's life was in danger. I immediately increased his daily dose of antidepressant and had him call me once or twice each day.

He did not want to die. He wanted reassurance that there could be an end to this pain without having to end his life. He was able to rely on my reassurance that I had been where he was, and there was hope.

His early life had been a painful struggle growing up in Korea, later coming to the United States, struggling with poverty and isolation. He was now widely recognized in his field.

At first medication only improved his sleep, but that provided him at least eight hours of relief, for which he was grateful. He seemed to be encouraged by my telling him about my own experience with depression and my recovery from it. After ten days he felt his depression beginning to lift.

Resistance to Medication

Many people, like Chad and myself suffer needlessly for years with emotional pain, reluctant to take medication for many reasons. We hate the idea of becoming dependent on it. We believe we should "tough it out" on our own. When we finally, reluctantly, agree to take medication, as in Chad's case, we often do not take enough to adequately treat our symptoms.

Skepticism about Medications

Many patients (and some therapists) have one major concern. What if the patient becomes addicted to the medication? The fear is that medication, even if used in a judicious way, will interfere with therapy and produce its own addiction.

Fear of addiction to medications is a growing concern among physicians and patients, ignited in alcohol and drug treatment centers where all mind-altering medications are grouped together. Horror stories about the results of misuse of medically prescribed drugs abound, fueled by a sensationalist media. There is rampant prejudice that people who use medication during the Restoration phase of healing are in grave danger of becoming addicts. This fear originates in the belief that addiction is in the medicine itself, or that it is simply a physiological problem.

Some medications we use during this phase are "clinically addicting." Benzodiazepines (including Xanax, Ativan, and Klonopin), used to treat anxiety and panic, are examples. Our nervous system becomes accustomed to them and too sudden discontinuation or abrupt withdrawal can produce severe symptoms. Very few people, though, develop a dangerous tolerance that requires increased dosage for relief of symptoms to these drugs. But these very useful medications suffer condemnation because of the few people who do develop tolerance, or who, as a result of being taken off these agents too quickly (usually in drug and alcohol treatment centers where insurance programs only allow hospital stays of a month or less), report having difficulties. With proper medical or psychiatric supervision, the few patients who do develop tolerance, can be quickly recognized and treated with complete success.

In my own experience, both personally and professionally, the advantage of alleviating debilitating pain far outweighs the difficulty or symptoms involved when these medications are discontinued.

Patients are sometimes emotionally brutalized in alcohol and drug treatment centers because of an antimedication bias. As I write, more physicians are becoming caught in the antidrug furor as part of the current "drug war" and are reluctant to use adequate medication to treat their patients. Fears of criticism or malpractice suits interfere with concern for the patient. Many programs, directed at substance-abuse addictions, lack balance; patients are treated "by the book" rather than by their individual needs. I realize we live in an imperfect world but I want to encourage any patients who have emotional symptoms to seek out physicians who offer balanced programs, programs which address medication as part of a healing program.

A Lack of Balance

The same lack of balance is painfully evident in psychiatry, where we are hampered by schools of psychiatry with diverse allegiances and beliefs. Biological psychiatrists, for example, would immediately think of antidepressants for a patient like Shelly who would respond as she did with my prescription. But they would overlook factors in Shelly's life (dating back to childhood) which underlie her depression and pain. Treated only with medication, she would enjoy a brief respite from her symptoms, but would likely have a recurrence or require indefinite medication.

When you integrate the work for changing beliefs with these other approaches, neither continued psychotherapy nor continued medication are necessary.

At another extreme are professionals like ones Shelly consulted before coming to us. They treated her physical pain (not the emotional roots), addressed her childhood issues in psychotherapy (using an analytical or dynamic model of psychotherapy), but overlooked her deep, chronic, nearly fatal depression.

Both Shelly's and Chad's stories illustrate for us the importance of the Restoration phase of the healing journey. They are not cured; they continue to face issues in therapy and in healing, admitting they are powerless over their pain, powerless over other people in their lives whom they have always striven to please. With the help of proper medication, though, they are able to deal with life issues adequately, and thus continue their healing. Medication reduces our pain, when that pain threatens to overwhelm us. But perhaps even more important it allows us to hope again, to rally the enthusiasm we need to continue with the healing journey that will ultimately make our lives happy and worthwhile.

Current Medications

There are two major classes of medications we most frequently use for treating people who are suffering from emotional addictions. These are antidepressants and antianxiety drugs. Sometimes it is necessary to combine these two categories of drugs to treat certain disorders.

Understanding Depression

The effective treatment of depression and other mood disorders began around 1940 with the introduction of electroconvulsive therapy (ECT). Before that time, there were really no effective treatments for people suffering depression or manic-depressive (bipolar) disorders. Electrical stimulation with ECT produces convulsions which somehow, often dramatically, relieve symptoms. Prior to the use of this primitive treatment, people were often committed for life to state financed asylums, where the average stay was between six months and five years.

Then, throughout the 1950s, sedatives such as phenobarbital, or bromide type drugs were used to treat manic behavior. Stimulants, including amphetamines, were used to treat depression. None of these drugs were satisfactory, and most were physically addictive.

The Antidepressant Drugs

These drugs currently fall into three major categories: Tricyclics, MAOI inhibitors, and Serotonin enhancers.

All three groups affect substances in the brain, brain hormones called neurotransmitters, which affect moods. The two major neurotransmitters involved in depression are noradrenalin and serotonin.

The most widely accepted theory is that depression occurs when one or both of these neurotransmitters is in short supply. This can occur from long-term stress, genetic deficiency, or some combination of these factors. Tricyclics prevent one or both neurotransmitters from being broken down. Thus, tricyclics can be used while the body is, presumably, manufacturing more neurotransmitter. Ultimately, the body will "catch up" and the drugs can be discontinued.

Another medication, lithium carbonate, is a salt chemically similar to table salt. I have used it in my practice since 1968 as a treatment for manic-depressive (Bipolar) disorders. Lithium effectively puts a "governor" on the racing thoughts and frantic activity of manic patients.

The drugs affect noradrenalin and serotonin in differing proportions. Some affect one or the other. Some effect both. There are to date no scientific tests to clearly determine which of these drugs will be effective in a particular person. Often combinations of these medications, or use with lithium and sometimes small amounts of thyroid or other medications are helpful in the Restoration process.

Side Effects of Antidepressants

These medications produce the desired effects of relieving depression and sometimes anxiety. They also produce side effects that are not pleasant. Dry mouth, constipation, tremor, urine retention, rapid heart rate, increased perspiration, and light-headedness are the most common side effects. Also, for little-known reasons, the drugs often take two to three weeks before providing relief. The MAOI drugs require certain food and dietary restrictions as well. The newer serotonin enhancers are remarkable because they often have fewer side effects than the other, older drugs.

And the good news is that if they work once, they generally will work again if depression recurs.

Understanding Anxiety

In 1977, there was a breakthrough in scientific research, providing us with a deeper understanding of the biochemistry of anxiety. Researchers found in the brain an inhibitory hormone, called GABA, which regulates anxiety.

When there is a shortage of this substance in the brain, we experience anxiety. As a result of these discoveries, anxiety and panic disorders are now categorized as chemical or biological problems.

A number of drugs were developed to operate within this system to reduce the symptoms of panic and anxiety. The first of these were Librium and Valium, both benzodiazepines. Early in their history, these drugs were over-prescribed and misused. Thus they won for themselves a very bad reputation, particularly in the public eye. Part of the difficulty had to do with the fact that these early drugs remained in the body for a longer period of time than most other drugs of this type. Withdrawal from them is prolonged and can be quite uncomfortable if not properly managed. This last point is perhaps the most important in treatment—the proper management of the withdrawal of the drug as the person changes and no longer requires its use.

The benzodiazepines have been improved considerably, and in their new forms offer effective relief with minimal side effects and dangers. The three modern versions of these drugs are alprazolam (Xanax), lorazepam (Ativan) and clonazepam (Klonopin).

Profiles of Three Modern Antianxiety Drugs

Alprazolam (Xanax). While in the same chemical class as Valium, alprazolam has a somewhat different chemical structure, avoiding the problems of its earlier counterparts. It is particularly effective in the treatment of panic attacks. In studies where this drug was carefully managed, it blocked panic attacks completely in 85 percent of the people who took it. My experience with my own patients is even

146 • *Magnificent Addiction*

better than that, with relief from panic attacks reported in more than 97 percent of the cases where I prescribed it.

Lorazepam (Ativan). This is similar to alprazolam in its ability to relieve anxiety and, in many instances, panic. Both lorazepam and alprazolam remain in the body a relatively short period of time (four to six hours). They must be taken several times a day to block anxiety and panic.

Clonazepam (Klonopin). This is a longer-lasting drug than either of the above and is effective for both anxiety and panic attacks. Since it has a longer life in the body, it can be particularly helpful for people whose sleep is disturbed as the result of panic attacks. Taken only twice a day, a person can set up a medication program that allows sleep through the night, free of panic or anxiety.

Side Effects

The biggest complaint that most people have with these drugs is short term memory loss. For example, a person might forget a phone number or the name of another person. Again, when we discontinue the use of these drugs, we need to do it with caution. The brain cells become accustomed to them and the physical symptoms of withdrawal can be experienced unless the process of discontinuing the drug's use is intelligently managed.

Withdrawal from benzodiazepines can be a particular problem for people with a family history of alcoholism, and should be monitored by a physician who is familiar both with the management of the benzodiazepines and with procedures for prescribing them for alcoholics or with people from alcoholic families.

The benzodiazepines have received a great deal of negative attention in recent years. Most of this bad press has been the result of experiences at drug and alcohol treatment centers, where patients were put on these drugs in the "drying out" process from alcohol or street drugs. Problems arose when the prescription drugs were suddenly withdrawn at the end of the person's stay at the treatment center. In most cases, these programs last for 28 to 30 days. This is not enough time to manage both withdrawal from alcohol and withdrawal from the bensodiazepine.

For most people, the withdrawal symptoms are somewhat worse than those suffered by a person coming off heavy caffeine consumption. In very rare instances, grand-mal convulsions have been experienced when medication was suddenly stopped.

As imperfect as these drugs may be, they are a vast improvement over the drugs used to reduce anxiety in the 1960s and '70s. And certainly they are much, much less dangerous than alcohol, which is the most widely used substance for reducing anxiety.

The slogan, "progress, not perfection" is as applicable in the use of drugs as it is in 12-Step programs.

Duration of the Restoration Process

For most people the stages of healing overlap. Restoration, using medication and psychotherapy to alleviate painful and disabling symptoms, varies in length depending on individual needs and requirements. For most, the reparenting experience and reprogramming of beliefs begin almost immediately. For others, weeks or months of medication and psychotherapy are necessary before it becomes possible to focus on buried feelings and expose addictive beliefs.

Personal Experience with Medications

I learned a balanced approach through the experience of trial and error, both from years of trying to find better ways to help patients and from my own breakdown and healing. There was a time when I would have counted myself in the "antimedication" camp, too.

My personal search led me to explore many holistic, non-coventional, non-drug oriented treatments for emotional disease, both prior to and following recovery from my own breakdown. I viewed medication with skepticism and, like addiction, believed it was for someone else, not me. In treating depression, in particular, patients sometimes complained of uncomfortable side effects. I could easily understand their reluctance to follow my prescriptions. The cure sometimes seemed more painful than the disease. Their complaints, as well as my own awareness of the limited help medication provided, played a part in my continued searching for better answers.

Using Process or "feeling therapy" to treat all my patients was one such answer. In 1970, when I set up a three bedroom house in a residential neighborhood in San Diego as a "feeling center," I gave up doing everything else. No medication. No counseling. Nothing but "feeling to heal." Patients would arrive each morning at the center and stay all day, lying on foam pads with the instruction to feel their feelings without acting on them. I was so impressed with the early results of this new therapy that I fancied it would be the answer for all my patients. I discontinued using medication in my practice and devoted my entire time to exploring the power of feelings to heal everyone. One dramatic example changed my mind.

Evelyn was a pleasantly plump, thirty-four-year-old woman who always wore brightly colored outfits, had bright eyes and a frequent, machine-gun-like giggle. She was referred to the center by another patient of mine who was benefiting from the program.

Evelyn had been diagnosed as a paranoid schizophrenic and had recently been hospitalized twice because of hearing voices which accused her of being evil and directing her to kill herself. She also had a belief that she was here on earth with a mission to instruct other people about their beauty. Unfortunately pursuing this mission led her to neglect her husband and two small children, annoy her immediate neighbors and brought her to the frequent attention of the police. She would make "mission visits," as she called them, into the neighborhood preaching loudly, not concerning herself with whether or not she had a receptive audience.

She was being given powerful tranquilizers to control her symptoms. The drugs quieted her voices and allowed her to remain at home, functioning reasonably well. But she hated being on drugs, disliked the side effects of stiffness in her muscles, the distortion of her handwriting and the interference with her creative thinking that these medications produced. She showed me some poetry she had written in college and I was deeply touched. She said the drugs blocked these writings and she felt frustrated. She told me how she could not feel deep feelings anymore. Evelyn won me over. Despite what I learned of schizophrenia, despite all my earlier experience, when she talked about having problems with feelings, I became her advocate.

Following my instructions, Evelyn gradually reduced her dosage of medication until she was drug free. She would arrive each morning, lie down in her assigned place, and "feel feelings." It seemed to help for more than three weeks. (About as long as it took for the beneficial effects of medication to wear off after they were discontinued.)

One morning she walked into the living area wearing nothing more than her bright smile, accompanied by her rat-a-tat giggle. She wanted to offer her nude body as a demonstration to the world that "the human body is beautiful." Her sense of mission had returned in full force. I protested, argued, discouraged, and reasoned—all to no avail. I was unable to convince Evelyn that her planned march through this sedate residential neighborhood was not a good idea. She walked outside, while I stood helplessly in the doorway, and headed down the sidewalk, striding proudly ahead to do her work.

Thirty minutes later a police cruiser circled the block, pulled up outside my center and stopped. Two uniformed police officers gently escorted Evelyn, now wrapped in a heavy blanket, inside. She sat glaring angrily ahead. Her face was flushed and she was not giggling. She was still unyielding, steadfastly convinced of her mission.

I felt awful. I was embarrassed—for Evelyn and myself—and was asking myself how I could have done anything so foolish as to believe that feeling feelings could ever be powerful enough to cure schizophrenia. If wanting her well would have helped, Evelyn would have been cured. But it was not to be. I was suddenly and dramatically un-converted from my belief that feeling feelings could heal all ills—particularly Evelyn's. I asked the police if they would drive Evelyn to the psychiatric emergency room and called ahead to alert the psychiatrist there. She was restarted on her medication and her symptoms resolved in a few days.

What I failed to account for in my fervor for this new therapy was that Evelyn and other people labelled schizophrenic, as well as patients with depression, panic attacks, phobias, obsessive-compulsive disorders, and many psychosomatic disorders have what must be considered, chronic disorders with long-term changes in their thinking, beliefs, and habits as well as their personalities and internal chemistry. These chronic conditions require remedies more powerful than a brief exposure to feeling feelings or any other single psychiatric or psychological method can generate.

When my breakdown struck, I explored using amino acids (phenylalanine, L-tryptophan, and tyrosine) which are building blocks of the brain hormones (serotonin and norepinephrine), believed to be involved in depression. I also looked into homeopathic remedies and certain herbs. I found them only minimally effective. In higher doses these had side effects too.

Eventually my experience convinced me that adequate dosage of proper medication is the best answer we have currently available for treating the symptoms of these chronic conditions.

Restoration through Psychotherapy

What about psychotherapy as a part of Restoration? I recall patients who were suicidal during their initial phone call to my office yet were much better when they came for their first visit. Studies show that many people begin to improve with their first contact with a helping person. Overcoming the incredible loneliness and shame surrounding emotional illness and merely reaching out for help can sometimes begin to restore people as effectively as medication.

Many other forms of psychotherapy can do this as well. If medication provides the pre-healing, then psychotherapy provides the "discovery" necessary for healing. Feeling understood, supported, and no longer alone in one's struggles can soothe the pain as powerfully as the best medication. Learning and understanding the connection between childhood experiences and our adult struggle can clear a lot of confusion. But generally not as quickly as medication. Furthermore, there are clearly times when the symptoms are too chronic and too deep for psychotherapy.

If we lived in an ideal world, supported with generous trust funds, and if we could all leave our stressful jobs and return to the rustic countryside, we would undoubtedly require much less medication or psychotherapy. But the world is less than perfect. Most of us are in jobs where we are constantly pressured to perform, to cope with daily aggravations which would test the patience of a saint. We live in a world where time is valuable, and we cannot take weeks or months to get over the painful feelings that are crippling us.

Once our symptoms are adequately treated, psychotherapy can be more effective. Timing is everything. Many psychiatric patients are told they must stay on medication for their entire lives. Others who attend some 12-Step meetings or consult holistic healers are advised to throw away their drugs. What I am trying to teach and practice is balance.

What's the Answer?

Balance is crucial in every treatment program. Too rigid a position in either direction—no medication or primarily medication—vastly limits the chances for change and total recovery. Medications are crucial for easing pain, restoring strength, and giving us hope. But they do not change the root causes of those symptoms, which continue to live within us, whether we're receiving medication or not, until we choose to address them.

How do we address the root causes and free ourselves of them? That's the subject of the next two chapters—reparenting ourselves, and reprogramming beliefs.

REPARENTING OURSELVES

Who among us has not searched or is not still searching for a perfect relationship? A nearly flawless person who is romantic and passionate, who will understand us completely, love us unconditionally, listen to us patiently without advising or interrupting, and not only care for us ,without complaining, but tolerate our moodiness and shortcomings while asking for little or nothing in return. No doubt I exaggerate a bit, but certainly this is not unlike the fantasy I held for many years and the one many of my patients have. Most of us harbor a wish for someone nearly this ideal. One of my patients described this person as "an ideal parent with sex privileges."

The wisdom and humility that grows out of a breakdown, whatever its cause, dramatically alters this picture. We become concerned with merely surviving then and learn to accept that there is no such person. If there were, and he or she provided us with all we fantasized, we would still sometimes feel depressed and lonely and experience a deep emptiness as we do now. And we would resume seeking to quiet our pain in much the same ways we do now—after a honeymoon period. The pain of breakdowns directs us inside in our search for answers. One good result is that our feelings and intuitions become our guides and we finally give up our fantasies. Pain is a powerful attention grabber. What begins as pain grasps and holds

~~our undivided attention. It serves us by changing our focus from~~ looking outside for ideal relationships or solutions to a search for answers within ourselves.

One answer that became clear for me during my breakdown and healing is that we can learn to offer the qualities that we seek in an ideal relationship to ourselves. Not only can we become the ideal emotional parent that we are looking for in model relationships, but we are, in fact, the only person who can accomplish this.Perhaps the poet Elizabeth Barret Browning loved her husband Robert so completely ("How do I love thee? Let me count the ways") but most of us must reparent ourselves. We are left with wounds that are too ancient and too deep for others, who are wounded too, to heal us. We have frequently lost the ability to trust others or our faith in them is so weak that our relationships are marred by constant "tests," whose inevitable failure will cause us to withdraw once more into ourselves.

How can we learn to reparent ourselves? First, we learn to become aware of and focus on our feelings. This is accomplished by allowing ourselves to experience thoughts, feelings, and physical sensations in our bodies without judgment or constraint and without trying to control, get rid of, or change any of them. In this way we learn to allow our emotions to guide us inward to uncover buried feelings from the past or to reveal the beliefs that underlie our feelings. Accepting our feelings without judging them as good, bad, right, or wrong is a means to become our own emotional parents. By learning this we become less dependent emotionally on others, a process called "individuation" (discussed in Chapter 13) and begin a process of learning to love ourselves unconditionally. Unconditional love is the love that heals us.

There are three major steps in this process:

1. Awareness

Learning to focus or direct attention on what is occurring inside us. We gently notice each thought, feeling, and bodily sensation.

2. Permission

Allowing ourselves to think each thought (even distracting ones from the outside) or feel each feeling, as it occurs, without judgement and without trying to control the feeling in any way. We allow thoughts or feelings to stay as long as they choose to stay.

3. Letting Go

Lovingly deepen the experience of steps 1 and 2 by continuing to accept each thought, feeling, or sensation unconditionally until it chooses to go away or change itself. Give over control to thoughts and feelings.

This simple three-stage process, offering acknowledgment and unconditional acceptance of our thoughts and feelings, teaches us to love ourselves. Notice that no action is involved on our part. We simply become aware of and "feel" our feelings without acting on them. Living this way—loving and accepting our feelings unconditionally—allows us to become the emotional parent(s) we always wished we had.

I never think about reparenting without recalling Beth, an attractive twenty-eight-year-old who "exploded" into my waiting room without an appointment.

She simply told my receptionist that she would "wait" when told I was busy. She did. I found her a charming combination of warmth and fear. And her determination to see me that day, with no delays, overrode any thoughts I might have had about taking a break for lunch.

Picture a child's face on a tall, athletic-looking woman's body, dressed in clothes that spoke of 1950s hand-me-downs. Imagine energy that expanded everywhere in the vicinity of her presence and you have some sense of Beth.

She was irritated and frightened by the return of crippling panic attacks which had forced her to give up many of her activities—her job, transporting her children, seeing her friends, and most important to her, going to church. She was deeply spiritual. She had turned to God years earlier after marrying a heroin addict at sixteen. He had died from an overdose, leaving her with a daughter to raise alone.

Now remarried, she had two other small children and a husband who was more child than adult. She felt trapped and overwhelmed. Beth could see the contradiction between her trust and belief in God and these uncontrollable attacks when she feared dying. But she was

~~powerless in trying to stop these attacks, even when she turned to~~ prayer.

She was impatient to begin work with me at that moment. She reluctantly agreed to start medication. However, she finally decided to do so and got relief from her panic in the first 24 hours. However, she was not satisfied. She hated drugs. She felt that they had caused her pain and she wanted to work on her healing without drugs.

"What do I need to do?" she asked.

I told her that her panic was the result of her fear of her own feelings—feelings that she could not control. If she was willing to feel her feelings without time limits or compromise she could desensitize herself to these them and the panic attacks would disappear.

"If you have the time and the guts, I suppose you can heal this in a single lengthy session," I told her, never dreaming how she would react to my words.

We made a tape recording of a visualization process I use in helping people with panic accomplish this desensitization. She took the tape and left.

I didn't hear from Beth for more than two months. I assumed the medication was helping her and that relistening to the tape was helping her begin to desensitize her fear.

I was not prepared for her next explosion into my office. This time she called ahead for an appointment.

She looked wonderful. She had gained a few pounds. Her childlike face glowed, and she reminded me of paintings of the Madonna that I remember hanging in Catholic schools. She wore a bright linen suit that made her look like an executive from a modeling school. She couldn't wait to begin.

"Well, I did what you said," she told me. "I went home, threw out the medication and just stayed in my room and 'felt my feelings.' I must have listened to that dumb tape a hundred times. But you were right. It did go away. I have never felt better. I have my usual fears but that creepy panic crap is gone. I just couldn't wait to tell you."

Beth had undertaken this process of feeling her feelings with unparalleled vigor. The process allowed her to begin becoming desensitized to her panicky fears. She was accepting her feelings and allowing them to be. She was reparenting herself and learning to love herself (and her feelings) unconditionally.

Healing the Inner Child

Looking upon our emotions as our inner child has become a popular and useful metaphor to visualize and express the process of reconnecting with our emotions. The inner child is a useful image in the healing process. Feelings are most often associated with childhood. As a result of being battered by life's experiences, we toughen and often lose easy access to our feelings.

We may look in the mirror and say, "I have no identity. I don't know who I am." I think this quandary results from separation from true feelings. Children seldom ask those questions. They still have access to their feelings because they haven't learned to bury them yet.

Separation from feelings begins early for many of us. Often we can trace painful feelings to childhood. In doing so, we recall the same feelings—in the same places in our bodies—that we had as kids. Later, as we heal, we can trace happier feelings from childhood in the same way.

Learning about Feelings

Our most difficult task is to teach people about feelings. When we are able to recognize, identify, and experience feelings, healing can progress quickly. Why is it so difficult for people to reach this point?

Feelings are natural and essential for survival. But often we are "conditioned" to experience them only indirectly. We may have learned that the only way we can express them is as physical symptoms. In extreme cases we are taught to experience them not at all. In order for any society to survive, individuals must learn certain rules and customs which subordinate their own feelings to the personal wishes and needs of others. Within limits, this is useful and necessary. But problems arise for individuals when symptoms develop, when our wishes and needs are subordinated not for the good of society but for the apparent good, or simply convenience, of a parent or other significant person in our early lives. The addictive patterns that lead to symptoms result from this process. Childhood is our earliest experience of brainwashing. Our learning creates our beliefs, and our beliefs affect our emotions. If these beliefs include denying and suppressing emotions (a natural survival tool), then the seeds for disorders and unhealthy addiction are sown.

Many people are raised by unhappy, frightened parents. Childhood is then spent in an effort to make this unhappy or frightened parent feel better. The primary joy of childhood is to be a child. When this is not possible, a pattern is established which becomes the norm for relating to everyone.

A child who has spent his or her early life pleasing others grows up to be a "people pleaser," a very painful addiction. Each year they live this way they become less and less able to connect with their own feelings, and finally experience a complete loss of self, where they really do not know "who they are."

Living a Role versus Real Living

The greatest tragedy is to live a role instead of living our own life. We learn roles. We play games with clear rules, instead of being ourselves. Recognizing this, hundreds of books cram the "how-to" market. Their solutions, though, only go so far. The real solution is simple, but the process is difficult and requires much more than understanding the problem. Abstract knowledge alone is not enough. An awareness of feelings is necessary in order to proceed toward healing.

The Real Power Is Within

The major problem in "role living" is that we place the power to be happy, content, peaceful, and serene under the control of other people. We give away our power. Properly, the source of our power to be happy is within ourselves. What we think and feel about ourselves is really what is important, not what someone else thinks or feels about us.

We have learned how to give our power to parents and other authorities, and then we become addicted to that pattern. After doing this we must have the approval of others in order to feel okay.

And since we are constantly judged as "okay" or "not okay," we do the same to others: we judge, compare, and "understand" them.

This judging forms the basis for conditional love—the "I will love you if you do such and so" syndrome. We learned that in order to be loved, we must meet conditions of making or keeping someone else happy. We practice what we were taught. So the same pattern of role living goes on and on. Our lives are always "dependent" because we continue to place the responsibility for our happiness outside ourselves. In order for us to love others, they must meet our "conditions."

Our Body's Instruction Manual

Paying attention to our feelings can teach us most of what we need to know about ourselves and what course to take in most of our actions. As our early warning system, our wake-up alarm, our feelings are the best gauge of what is best for us.

Recognized and listened to, our feelings can lead us to the answers about who we are and what we want. When we fail to uncover our real feelings they remain disguised, buried inside, and leading to dis-ease, as I described earlier. Feelings are our closest friends, our children, our lovers, our most intimate selves, but when they remain disguised or ignored, they can destroy our bodies and ultimately our lives.

Therapists, teachers, parents, friends, lovers, and even strangers, can help us begin to trust our feelings. (Note, the emphasis is not on trusting these people, but on using them to learn to trust ourselves.) They can serve as role models for caring about our selves. They can help restore hope and trust, that it is safe to experience our feelings directly. They can be our bridges to healing. Yet bridges are passive tools. Nothing happens unless we cross them.

Other people can help us discover the connection with our lost or buried feelings. There are many approaches that direct us inside to discover the sources of our pain and learn that it is safe to trust. What we really learn, though, is that trust must begin with trusting ourselves.

The power to heal comes from within.

Discovering Our True Feelings—Process

I call the technique I use to discover true feelings "Process." Not "Process Therapy" just Process. It is purposely a noun and a verb. It is a form of focused attention or awareness. It is a meditation on ourselves—our own thoughts, feelings, and inner experiences.

This model was developed over several years beginning in 1970. I spent thousands of hours over five years observing people "feeling their feelings" in the small rooms of the Process Center. In 1972 I moved the Center to a ranch north of San Diego surrounded by fields of multicolored flowers and clean ocean air. There was a comfortable guest house and two small apartments on the property which covered nine acres. My patients would stay in the apartments for three weeks and live a monklike existence. The purpose was to remove as many distractions as possible from the focus on "feelings". They would lie or sit alone for hours—sometimes 8–10 hours a day during their stay. My only instruction—since I was trying to direct them into themselves—was "notice and feel your feelings without taking any action on them."

Penny was an only child, now married with two small children. She had an aging, unhappy mother who called her daily to complain about her life. Penny felt angry, yet she felt too guilty to change the relationship for fear of hurting the old woman's feelings. She was referred to me because of panic attacks and severe depression which had gradually increased. She had been active in Alcoholics Anonymous for five years when I met her. Her concern about her addictive tendencies had made her reluctant to see a psychiatrist because she was afraid that even the prescription drugs for her symptoms might compromise or threaten her sobriety. When she became housebound from fear, had panic attacks even in her home, and could not sleep for fear of having an attack, she agreed reluctantly to consultation and treatment.

She did require medication. Her crippling symptoms made any exploration of her feelings impossible. She was in too much pain to concentrate on anything but her symptoms until she was medicated. Both antidepressants and antianxiety medications were required. After a few weeks she felt much better, began sleeping, and felt much less fearful. Her improved sleep alone seemed to reduce many of her other symptoms. She became well enough to leave the house, began driving, and was introduced to Process after twelve weeks.

She responded dramatically. One day she brought this account of her experience to her session.

> In the beginning, Process was mainly getting in touch with my feelings. This was difficult since I was unaware of them because I had stuffed them all my life. What I discovered while going through Process was that my fear was much worse than feeling my feelings was. I could see I would survive and actually benefit from this.
>
> To Process I close my eyes and go inside. Dr Kavanaugh guides me back to childhood, to the little girl inside. I grew up in a dysfunctional family and the feelings I had stuffed begin to surface— the pain and anger of that little girl. I surrender to the energy of these feelings. I almost become the feelings since everything else ceases to exist for that time period. That was the first step for me.
>
> The second part of Processing is visualizing that little girl, holding her on my lap, nurturing her, reparenting her, giving her the love and attention she needs. I give myself what was lacking from my parents. I can move on instead of staying stuck in that pain and anger. I can move towards becoming a whole person.
>
> An example occurred in a recent therapy session. I was feeling guilty and inadequate as a parent. I had been short-tempered with my children and I felt I wasn't giving them as much of my time and self as I should. I processed this guilt and sadness and went back to the little girl inside me who is still so needy. I was able to visualize the little girl in me. I was able to hold and love and cherish her, give her what she needed many years ago. I can actually feel the healing taking place inside me.
>
> The result was that I had compassion for myself as a parent. I was able to nurture myself and then I forgave myself. How could I give the kids something I didn't have? By processing and learning to take care of myself emotionally, I am able to heal a few pieces of the child inside me. Now I feel more able to give to my own children.

This illustrates several features of this "feel to heal" method. Penny became aware of her feelings and gave herself permission to feel them. She learned to observe, accept, and love her "inner children"—her feelings. She is reparenting herself emotionally when she is able to nurture her inner child. Then she is able to give freely and lovingly to her children.

Today, 12-Step recovery is popular, and this child-self is considered an inner divinity—a God self within. For some, making this "connection" after years of medication, unrewarding therapy, and complete loss of hope can be life saving. There are people with varying degrees of dis-ease who can use this powerful tool. Some, like Beth, require only an invitation and a nudge in the right direction. Others have deeper scars, far less trust in anyone (especially themselves), and reach the point of attempting suicide before they can turn within themselves for these answers.

I met Kathy by accident, but our connecting and the timing for us later convinced both of us that this was one of those planned accidents that was "meant to happen" when it did.

One Sunday evening she came into the emergency room at Good Samaritan Hospital where I am a staff psychiatrist. I was passing through that area after visiting a friend of mine. One of the Emergency Room physicians I know asked if I would see this "mess" who had come in after trying unsuccessfully to kill herself by running a hose from her exhaust pipe into her car and starting the engine. Only a chance visit from her brother, who lived in Alaska and was between planes in San Jose, prevented her attempt from being an actual suicide. Her psychiatrist had called after learning about her suicide attempt (this was her fourth) and had asked that the staff try to find someone else to work with her.

He was burned out on Kathy. My wife was away for a week and I felt interested by the challenge of this impossible patient. She was as near death as I have ever seen anyone be without dying. She was lying semi-conscious on a gurney, unable to talk, and headed for three days in Intensive Care. I stayed for nearly half an hour just talking out loud, never sure she could hear me, saying just what I felt she must have felt when she decided to do this.

She had not left a note. She looked almost childlike on the gurney. I could only make out the outlines of a tiny, frail-looking body. Her skin was flushed from the carbon monoxide; her lips were dry and chapped. But she had the most beautiful dark hair, which was the only part of her which seemed unaffected by her suicide attempt.

In the waiting room her husband Matt and their son Matt Jr., were sitting in a corner alternately crying and holding each other. They both were at a loss to explain what had led to this attempt—the most serious by far. She had seemed happier than usual lately.

Kathy had been seeing psychiatrists for years. She had been depressed after Matt Jr., now eleven, was born. She had taken antidepressants. This was followed by three years of analysis of the details of her Irish, Catholic, Alcoholic childhood (a trio I fondly call the "blessed trinity"). Her first suicide attempt occurred when Matt Jr. was six. She spent two months in the hospital and two more years of psychotherapy.

At one point Matt and she devoted a year to marriage counseling. Later it was felt she was not aggressive enough; so, assertiveness training classes were begun. Her lack of a college education seemed an issue according to her therapist, and she enrolled in junior college. Nothing seemed to touch the core of Kathy's depression. She never seemed "up" for long. And I noted that she was always the "recipient" of the therapy. Matt constantly referred to the therapists' opinions, never mentioning what Kathy thought or felt.

She made her second suicide attempt toward the end of this therapy. Her family had certain "classic" features as well. Her mother still denied her dad's alcoholism and still referred to him as a "good provider." Two of her four brothers were alcoholics, and one was a missionary priest in South America. Her only sister was a nun in the Carmelite Order where she had taken a vow of silence and never saw her family except through a screen.

Kathy had been a model child and her dad's favorite. She was the only one, according to her later account, that he had never hit. Life was chaotic with frequent times of uproar around her dad's binges. There was lots of financial insecurity because he lost jobs as a carpenter when he failed to show up for work. She felt shame and embarrassment about this. She had considered entering the convent during high school like her sister did later. Instead, she had met Matt, who attended another Catholic high school nearby, at a dance after a basketball game, and was smitten. She was sixteen. Matt, two years older, was her first boy friend, and she never dated anyone else until they married four years later. They never fought.

Now, at thirty-three, she was near death in the emergency room. Her first emotion when she became fully conscious two days later was embarrassment—then anger. Anger at God who "made me live" and anger toward herself at the failure of this carefully planned attempt (she had arranged everything when her husband and son were at a church camping weekend).

She listened to me but refused to talk, saying over and over, "It's no use. I can never be happy." She was transferred to the locked psychiatric unit and placed under close supervision. Despite that she seemed hell bent on suicide. She even tried drowning herself in the toilet when all sharp objects were removed from her room.

She continued to resist conversation. Not wanting to be bored, I would talk to her. I told her stories. I told her stories that had delighted my kids years earlier, about smart kids and dumb adults. My children used to love to hear chapter after contrived chapter of a story of kids triumphing over big people. I would lightly disguise their names. Amy would be Amia, Judy, Judia and Liz, Lizia. Kathy, of course, was Kathia.

She remained mostly mute during my stories. Later she turned away yet I knew she was listening because I could see her body tense when I would stop at an exciting point in one of the stories.

I learned from Matt that she loved animals, so I always worked small, helpless cats and dogs, injured deer and abandoned bear cubs throughout the stories. And it finally worked. One day, hearing how the mean trapper snared three tiny little bear cubs and dragged them over the rocks and brush, she started to cry. Later when Kathia constructed a trap for the trapper and snared him by his private parts, she laughed. I knew then that Kathy was going to recover. And she did.

She asked me to tell that story again and again, just as my kids had, and she began to cry as much as I have ever seen anyone cry. She literally cried for weeks. Later, at home, she continued crying, then opened to the stories behind her tears. Those bear cubs were the three youngest in her family—herself, her priest brother, and her cloistered nun sister who had been "trapped" and sexually abused by their mother's brother for years. She had never told anyone—not Matt, not her therapists, not even the priest in confession. She didn't tell me for months either.

Slowly Kathy connected with the beautiful abused child she had buried who was angry, guilty, and ashamed. She connected with the child within whom she had tried so often to kill rather than feel; to punish rather than nurture; to condemn rather than forgive and understand. She could only imagine a world of harsh judgment like the one she had known as a child.

It was this experience that helped Kathy connect with her feelings. Our months of work together helped her believe that her little girl, who loved animals, was more—that she was somehow divine, worthy of miracles, and truly worthy of the God within her.

The Components of Process: Awareness, Permission, Letting Go

Let's examine the Process step by step.

Step One: Awareness

Awareness is the core of Process. Continuous tuning into thoughts, feelings, and bodily sensations and granting them our permission to exist are the essential steps in reparenting ourselves. A direct connection to our inner child. When we seek answers "out there," using drugs, behaviors, or relationships for our "fix," we avoid our inner feelings. Or we try to change them.

Exercise # 1

Begin by creating a proper environment to tune in to your feelings. Sit or lie quietly and "observe" yourself. This means simply noting what is taking place inside your head and body. Practicing this alone without distractions (background music, supportive people nearby) is difficult at first. Try doing it for just a few seconds. Gradually extend practice sessions. In therapy sessions patients do this for hours.

Becoming aware of what's happening within ourselves reverses a lifetime of looking "out there" for love, reassurance and happiness and begins the reparenting process.

Step Two: Permission

Permission is an extension of awareness. We offer loving permission to each of our thoughts, feelings and physical sensations—without judgment, and without having to understand their meaning. We give ourselves permission to feel whatever we think or feel. Nothing is graded, regulated compared or criticized. Whatever we experience is simply allowed to be. This unlimited permission to "feel" is the essential element.

By granting ourselves this permission to feel the full range of our feelings, we prepare ourselves for unconditional love and acceptance. We choose not to control what we think or feel. Most of us have been taught, for instance, that feelings (such as love, joy, and happiness) are acceptable, while others (such as anger, fear, and guilt) are not. Here we give unrestricted permission to our feelings.

Many patients stall at this point because of guilt or shame about having certain feelings. They find it difficult to allow themselves to simply feel the guilt and shame. Or they may be afraid of other feelings. For example, patients who experience panic are "afraid to feel afraid" and resist or deny permission for themselves to feel fear. I have many times described myself and other psychiatrists as professional permission givers. Here I pass this permission on to you and teach you to become your own therapist—your own permission giver.

Feelings, as I emphasize repeatedly, are not moral or immoral. There are no right or wrong emotions. Our feelings are neutral. Only actions are right or wrong because actions have social consequences. We can have control over actions we take as a result of our feelings, but we cannot control feelings we have—they just are.

Actions have social consequences—emotions do not. Actions are right or wrong because they affect us or someone else. As a result, our actions should sometimes be restrained—feelings should not.

To grow emotionally, we must be able to observe ourselves totally—thoughts, sensations and feelings—without taking any action. While disguising and burying emotional energy as adults damages us, it is equally toxic to act out feelings rather than experience them.

When we act on feelings, their energy is changed. Talking, restless movements, exercise, drinking, smoking, working, and sex all alter our emotions. When we act rather than feel, we fail to develop emotional muscles. Experiencing feelings builds emotional strength just as lifting weights or aerobic exercise builds physical strength and stamina. The purpose of suspending action (and even thinking about feelings can be an action) is to help us have choices.

Feelings are neutral.

Exercise # 2

Picture yourself in a situation where you are full of anger and rage. For example think of an experience where you were hurt or belittled or embarrassed. Replay the experience as aggressively as you dare. Picture yourself having angry feelings, feel the anger if you can, but restrain from any action. Tell yourself that the feeling is not right or wrong. It's just okay to be. See if you can visualize how it would be to be given permission to feel totally without having to take any action. Is the feeling enough to satisfy? Does the anger disappear? (Remember, feelings are neutral.)

In Process we give ourselves permission to feel feelings. We stay with our feelings long enough to become "rational" or give ourselves time to "think through" our actions.

I cannot emphasize strongly enough that permission given in this reparenting process is specifically the permission to *have the feelings*. The decision to act or not act on those feelings depends on blending our feelings with our thoughts. This is "rational" living.

Step Three: Letting Go

Letting go is the third step in reparenting ourselves. Permission opens the door and letting go allows feelings to come inside.

Feeling feelings does not lead to craziness; resisting or trying to control the feelings does.

Letting go is a step of emotional acceptance. Permission is like having a marriage license while letting go is akin to actually getting married. We let go and release ourselves into the feelings. For example, most of us resist feeling fear, instead choosing to avoid, escape, deny, or act on fear—anything to avoid that awful, scary feeling. As we become aware of the fear (Awareness), we accept that it is okay to feel afraid (Permission), and then let ourselves have the fear (Letting

~~Go). Experiencing feelings, whether pleasant or painful, allows the~~ feelings to disappear. Again we feel to heal.

When we experience anxiety, this step requests us to move towards rather than away from the feeling. We invite feelings—even painful ones—to stay for lunch. We stay with the feeling, offering no resistance. Gradually the anxiety will fade away.

When we experience boredom, letting go means allowing ourselves to feel bored, staying with the bored feelings, offering no resistance and not doing anything to become unbored. Gradually boredom passes as we allow ourselves to feel it. This is true of other emotions as well. I often remind people that even the energy of good feelings fades. No doubt lottery winners even come back down to earth and the exhilaration first felt at the moment they heard they'd won passes.

If we feel any feeling long enough it will pass. After we let ourselves feel painful or uncomfortable feelings, peace and relaxation follow.

Awareness, permission, and letting go are steps that help us dissolve the barriers, defenses, and resistances we have built up presumably to protect ourselves from pain. Unfortunately these same barriers prevent us from accepting and loving ourselves unconditionally and becoming our own emotional parents.

Exercise # 3

Take a small photo of yourself as a child and spend time looking at it. Look at the eyes of that child. Notice the tiny body. Try to let yourself feel the emotions of that little boy or girl. Close your eyes and imagine that this child is still living inside you. Picture the child. Softly call the name you were called as a child. Say "(your name) I love you." Say it again. Let go and feel the feelings that arise. Then picture that tiny child coming and sitting on your lap. Feel him or her snuggling against you. Put your arms around that child and repeat "I love you." Next, picture yourself taking that child on a walk. Take that tiny hand in yours and go to your favorite peaceful place and sit sharing that place with your inner child.

Take this child with you in your car, next to you at work, on walks. Continue to visualize that child with you wherever you are.

Realize that you are not alone. You have your inner child. Before making decisions, ask your child what he or she wants or needs. Honor the feelings of that child within. You are not alone. This is the child you "buried" so many years ago when you began to look "out there" for love and reassurance. This exercise will help you reconnect with your inner child. Continue this exercise on a daily basis.

These three steps make up a form of self-meditation. We focus on our selves and our feelings. This is not selfish. We learn from this process that the natural desire we have once we have taken care of our inner child is to share what we have with others. I believe the natural outcome of this inner healing is the desire to love others. I believe this process allows us to connect with our inner child—our divinity. The child within and the God within are the same.

Reinforcement

We must reinforce what we learn. Daily practice helps us overcome deeply imbedded attachments, habits, and beliefs. We challenge and change our old beliefs by this process. Old fears will return unless we reinforce the new beliefs over and over again.

Behavior patterns and beliefs are so ingrained, automatic, and addictive that unlearning cannot take place without a long period of reinforcement. The lessons of this program are surrender and practice. We continue to surrender over and over. It is the task of a lifetime.

Many of us tend to feel we have a problem licked once we understand what it is. Understanding does not eliminate emotional problems. We must reinforce the changes into daily habits by constant repetition. We must make them part of our everyday lifestyle before they really make a difference in our lives.

Grief Is Part of Reparenting Ourselves

During reparenting, grief from buried and unfelt feelings is often reexperienced. We mourn the loss of a childhood we would have wanted ours to be. There is intimate sadness, and it is very common and natural to feel sorry for ourselves. We are like other animals who must heal by licking our own wounds. When we feel sorry for ourselves, this is accomplished.

Grief is one of the forbidden feelings. Memories of being told, "Stop feeling sorry for yourself," or "I'll give you something to feel sorry about!" are familiar and often vivid childhood memories for many of us.

Believe me, it is important to feel sorry for that child within in order to heal and recover. We grieve for that frightened, helpless child, grieve for the lost years, grieve for the missed nurturing. We grieve until the process of grieving is complete, until we have cried, mourned, and hurt for that child and sat and licked our wounds well, like an injured rabbit or deer.

Rewards of Reparenting Ourselves

This process reestablishes our connection between who we are and who we have tried to be, usually an actor or actress seeking love from others. Continuing to practice feeling feelings, and not acting on them (Process), allows this to occur. We experience ourselves, step-by-step, barrier-by-barrier, through the years. We wade through layers of buried grief, suppressed hurts, fears and anger, and penetrate the mantle of sensation, feeling, and emotions described above. We gradually reach a state of being emotionally open. We give up trying to control emotions. We simply have them.

The rewards are enormous. First we learn to immediately look within for answers when problems arise in our lives, not to others. As a result we become more self-reliant. We individuate (become our own, less-dependent, person). In the early years of guiding patients in this process, before I recognized and believed in a connection between the process of reparenting ourselves and our inner child, I believed self-integration accomplished by this method was life's highest achievement. Becoming connected with emotions and experiencing them without choosing to take any action was the ultimate goal of therapy. The later discovery that learning to nourish and love the tiny child within us through this approach is a way to love ourselves unconditionally dramatically changed my view of process. Here we discover more than our inner selves. We discover that we are able to love ourselves in a Godlike way. Here we connect with our divinity.

Connecting with ourselves in this way is a monumental accomplishment in healing. When we truly surrender to our feelings, we find our inner selves, we discover who we are. We discover that there is a unity within us, that we are human and divine. The acceptance and belief in this unity dissolves our fear. When indeed we are ourselves and God, there is no reason to fear. This is our reward. Feeling oneness, peace of mind, and serenity—characteristics of our inner spiritual Godness. I consider this the bonus for reparenting and cooperating with the miracle of spiritual healing—referred to as "grace." We do the footwork and God controls the outcome. The footwork in reparenting involves confronting the barriers we have erected and melting them by cooperating with the warmth of the healing grace of spirit.

Thus we learn to love ourselves unconditionally because we learn of our inner unity with God.

We Still Need Relationships?

Does reparenting ourselves mean we do not need relationships with other people? Not at all. It means that we are capable of having better, less dependent relationships. Most of us do better, have fewer accidents and illnesses, and live longer when we live in relationship. Too often, my patients have interpreted this idea of reparenting in a global way and assume that they must learn to live alone or end relationships that are not working. This is not true and reflects the "all or none" thinking of many of us from dysfunctional family backgrounds. It is important to become more self-dependent and less dependent on others during the reparenting process. We can learn to expect more of ourselves and less of our partner by practicing the steps of reparenting day by day in our lives.

In my experience, it has been quite clear that we can reparent ourselves best when we are in relationship. There, we can practice self-dependency and sustain a balance by creating a loving, give-and-take relationship. While we learn that our partner cannot be our substitute parent, it is often helpful to have the support of a loving partner while we undergo this difficult process of reparenting.

When I present the idea of reparenting ourselves to groups, I use the personal example of lying next to my wife and not reaching out for reassurance. At these times, I may be feeling anxiety, facing an uncertain day ahead, or simply restlessness. Often these are not feelings of warmth and affection. When this occurs I choose to feel the feelings and do not act on them. Some people gasp when I use this example. Others who understand realize I am recommending a path of becoming more emotionally self-reliant in this way. I am not talking about never reaching out. Rather, I use this example to show that any relationship, good or bad, can be a place to practice and extend our reparenting skills.

The more successfully we reparent ourselves, the less dependent we are in relationships, and the more we can give. The less we are afraid, the better our relationships. The fear of commitment reflects our dependency, our quest for parenting from others, our lack of reparenting skills and our need for a process such as this one.

While reparenting is enormously important as we move toward recovery, we are much more than our feelings. We discover as we go along, that healing is incomplete until we address certain issues around spirituality. As you move on to the next chapter, you'll discover a way of looking at the spiritual aspects of life that are quite different than any taught in church.

REPROGRAMMING OURSELVES SPIRITUALLY

The major task in healing is to recognize and change addictive beliefs. Anything else merely shifts the symptoms, of our unhealthy addictive thinking and offers temporary help; it does not address the underlying disease which is in our thinking. Such a shift only refocuses our addictive energy without allowing it to truly nurture and heal us. Treating only the symptoms in this way blocks the full expression of our creativity and remains a barrier in the healing process.

Healing involves more than the steps we have taken thus far. Growing toward emotional balance, becoming peaceful, and feeling healthy all require us to change the beliefs that underlie our suffering. In the last chapter we saw how we can replace unhealthy dependencies and become more self-reliant. We are about to discover beliefs that offer us peace of mind rather than temporary solutions followed by months or years of destructive enslavement.

We'll be exploring in this chapter:

1. How to unlearn or emotionally detach from our present addictive beliefs about feeling abandoned and compulsively needing to be in control. We accept that these ego-driven beliefs are the source of our pain.

~~2. How to change our beliefs gradually, most often guided by~~
our feelings and instincts as gentle, trustworthy expressions of our
inner voice, the voice of our feelings and intuition. Emotions are mirrors which reflect back to us what we believe. As we change our
thinking and beliefs we begin to experience peace in place of our
pain.

Reprogramming Ourselves

There are many systems of thought whose acceptance offers this
peace of mind. Many of them are associated with organized religion,
whose overtones we have discussed. Here I will describe two programs, the 12-Step program and A Course In Miracles, whose ideas
continue to serve as a guide for me, my patients, and many others
whose lives touch mine.

The 12 Steps

This program begins by addressing our master addiction and our
deepest fears, starting with admitting to our powerlessness in the
first step. In 12-Step programs we participate in a group of people
who are also recovering from addictive beliefs similar to our own.
Working with others like ourselves lessens our shame, guilt and
embarrassment and provides us with an effective way of dealing
with the feelings of isolation, loneliness, and low self-worth that we
may feel at this time. These steps are not intended to be taken alone
but rather in a group or with an experienced member or sponsor.

The steps are divided into three main groups:

The Surrender Steps

Steps 1–3 guide us to accept the reality of our lives by admitting
that we are powerless over some aspect(s), such as certain substances,
behaviors, beliefs, etc. These steps instruct us to let go of trying to
control what is uncontrollable by us. We are asked to acknowledge a
higher power (a power greater than our own ego), and relinquish
control of our lives (trust) to the care of that greater power (whether
we identify that power as being within us or outside ourselves).

Step 1. We admitted that we were powerless over _____(mention a specific addiction) and that our lives had become unmanageable. We use "our symptoms" in our program since we are dealing with mostly with people who have emotional disorders.

Step 2. We came to believe that a power greater than ourselves could restore us to sanity.

Step 3. We decided to turn our will and our lives over to the care of God as we understood Him.

These three steps help us recognize and accept that we are not able to solve our problem alone and that we can accept help from a power greater than ourselves. This is the beginning of changing our beliefs about control. We give over control. For some people, completing these three steps may take days, weeks or months. Others may be able to accept them easily. For most of us we must continue to work on letting go of control throughout our lives.

Feeling resistance to surrendering our will to a Higher Power is part of a general resistance to giving up control. If we are willing to turn our lives over to a stockbroker, or share our deepest secrets with a hairdresser, why do we recoil when God is mentioned? This is our ego's fear of relinquishing control.

The Action Steps

Steps 4–9 involve doing something about ourselves and our lives. Here we make a commitment to action. We are addressing the reasons for our shame, and the isolation which results, as well as our dishonesty in our relationships as we have attempted to control other people in some way.

Step 4. We made a searching and fearless moral inventory of ourselves.

This step involves a thorough written review of our lives, admitting where we made faulty choices, not only towards others, but toward ourselves. This inventory highlights our assets as well as our shortcomings. When we write such an inventory we are once more surrendering control. The intention is to stop trying to be someone we are not or cannot be. What a relief!

Step 5. We admitted to God, to ourselves, and to another human being the exact nature of our wrongs.

This step includes a formal reading or discussion of the written material from step 4 with a sponsor (a more experienced member of the fellowship) and allows for the feeling of being unique or different from others. This underlies the idea that breakdowns can be shared, which helps relieve these symptoms.

Step 6. We were entirely ready to have God remove all these defects of character.

Step 7. We humbly asked God to remove our shortcomings.

These steps indicate our willingness to acknowledge human weaknesses, poor choices (step 6), and to have the humility to ask to have them "taken away," (step 7). Implicit in these steps is our acceptance that we are unable to rid ourselves of these defects of character without outside assistance.

Steps 8 and 9 involve the action of forgiveness, which is the most important element in healing. We look inside, examine our own participation in creating and continuing our problems or symptoms, acknowledge anyone we believe we have harmed (including ourselves), and take whatever action is necessary to achieve peace. In these two steps we try to completely clear our conscience and repair all past concerns so we can live in the present moment. We clearly make the past the past by making amends and achieving forgiveness wherever possible.

Step 8. We made a list of all persons we had harmed and became willing to make amends to them all.

Step 9. We made direct amends to such people wherever possible, except when to do so would injure them or others.

Forgiveness is the key to healing. It is the ultimate step in letting go of control. During the reparenting phase we surrender to our feelings. Here we surrender our beliefs and let our higher self or God be the judge instead of us.

Traditional psychotherapy all too often helps us regain control rather than surrender it as we have seen earlier.

The Reinforcement Steps

Steps 10–12 recognize the persistent nature of addictions and are the foundation for lifelong extension of these belief-changing principles.

Step 10. We continued to take personal inventory and, when we were wrong, promptly admitted it.

This allows for the mistakes we are certain to make, recognizing that personal growth and freedom from addictions is a process not a discovery or insight, and that we will continue to evolve. Addictive patterns are ingrained, deep-seated habits that cannot be willed away. Under stress we all tend to revert to familiar patterns of thinking, feeling, and behaving.

Step 11. We sought, through prayer and meditation, to improve our conscious contact with God as we understood Him, praying only for knowledge of His will for us and the power to carry that out.

In this step we learn to let go of trying to control God. We begin to pray unconditionally, with no strings attached. This is in stark contrast to the way most of us learned to pray—for something—as a result of the abusive God of our culture. Here we are encouraged to cease praying for things and pray only for knowledge and power, not results.

Step 12. Having had a spiritual awakening as the result of these steps, we tried to carry this message to others, and to practice these principles in all our affairs.

The final step emphasizes what has long been known and taught, first as the Golden Rule, and subsequently in all the spiritual programs I know about. We are all joined and what we give to others we are really giving to ourselves. This is why life's deepest joy and satisfaction is always derived from selfless service.

A successful recovery in 12-Step programs involves learning to surrender our ego's control and find joy and freedom in the ultimate addiction, found by searching inside where our answers lie, then experiencing the joy of giving to others; in this way we are giving to ourselves.

Actions of Recovery.

The important actions suggested in these steps are:

1. Admit that we are unable to control or manage our lives where our addictions are concerned and surrender our will to that of a Higher Power as defined by ourselves.

2. Go within ourselves for our source of self-worth instead of looking to others.

3. Develop self-esteem by being honest with ourselves. Let go of trying to control other people in any way including trying to control what they think of us.

4. Learn to live in the present moment by letting go of the past by finding forgiveness for ourselves and others. In this way we can let go of guilt or resentments in our past and move on.

These twelve steps offer us the power to help ourselves change our beliefs, but they do this only because we give them that power. The steps are part of the mythology of recovery. We believe that they reflect truth. The steps themselves are not the answer; they are only tools, helpful in guiding us to the real answers which are within ourselves. I view them as bridges that we use temporarily as we grow and change.

Slogans of the 12 Steps

The major beliefs contained in the 12 Steps are expressed well in slogans such as "Live and let live" (let go of trying to control other people); "Turn it over" or "Let go, let God" (relinquish control to a higher power); "Progress, not perfection." (address all-or-nothing thinking so common in addictions). (See appendix for a complete list.)

I recommend that these slogans be written on small cards and carried in a purse or shirt pocket to help reinforce the beliefs taught by the 12-Step model.

To simplify taking the steps, there are numerous workbooks which ask focused questions. We have an excellent one called "Corridors of Light," compiled by members of our staff.

Getting "Hooked" on the 12 Steps

Some people do become "hooked" on 12-Step programs. Focusing on attendance at meetings and not seeming to apply the principles in daily life is not uncommon. There are petty grievances, jealousy, and cliques. Gossip and breaking anonymity of other members does occur. A kind of spiritual fundamentalism exists in some groups where outmoded ideas about using medication are espoused and harsh judgments of people on antidepressants or antianxiety drugs abound.

Becoming hooked on a 12-Step program is certainly preferable to an enslavement to alcohol, cocaine, debt, or any other of our former choices, and a major advance over sex or relationship addictions.

It is good to remind ourselves that life is a process where we "upgrade" our addictions gradually until we find the one addiction that heals us. Being temporarily "hooked" on 12-Steps is a vast improvement over our former choices.

A Course In Miracles

I knew about the Course for many years but resisted many of the ideas. Since then, I have been recommending it for anyone in recovery and as "post graduate" work for anyone who has completed a 12-Step program. It aims at thought reversal by changing our addictive beliefs, just as the 12-Steps do. The goal of the Course is to teach us to reverse our perceptions, which are false, and replace them with true knowledge. One of the first principles of the Course is that we *project* or make the world that we see; if we wish to change that world, we can do so by changing our thoughts and beliefs.

While the Course describes a spiritual approach to our lives, it is not affiliated with any church or organized group. Study groups gather informally throughout the world, with each group taking on it own character, largely determined by its particular participants. There is no membership, no dues to pay, and although religious words such as God are used, belief in a higher power is not essential. The only requirement is a willingness to change.

Some of the beliefs include the following:

1. The world we see is an illusion, no different than the dreams we have when we sleep. It is a waking dream.

2. Our illusory world is made up of our projections. Projection makes perception. We can let go of this view of the world and substitute a true view.

3. Each of us is a Son of God, and part of a universal Spirit. We are all God.

4. Since we see only illusions, and everyone is Divine, we cannot sin. Because we have bodies, which are also part of the illusion, we can make mistakes. Sin then is not a violation deserving of punishment, but an error needing to be corrected.

5. The method of changing our thoughts is to forgive. Forgiveness is central to the Course, as it is in 12-Step programs. In order to change our perceptions we let go of attack thoughts and grievances. We forgive everyone, including ourselves.

6. The Course does not allow for exceptions. We must forgive totally in order to have peace and joy. We forgive not because we are charitable but because what we see and judge is simply not true and a part of the illusion.

7. The Course recognizes only two emotions: love and fear. Fear is part of the illusion and reflects our belief that we are in control of our lives. Ultimately love is all there is, since fear is an illusion.

8. Removing the barriers we have erected to love (miracles) is the aim of the Course.

The history of A Course In Miracles is a fascinating one, worth repeating here because it introduces the reader to the principles in a personal way.

It began in 1965 when two psychologists on the faculty at Columbia University in New York combined in a joint effort (directed by their boss) to "find a better way" of looking at their lives. Neither Helen Schucman or William Thetford were spiritual. Helen described herself as an atheist and Bill called himself an agnostic.

Helen began having highly symbolic dreams and images coming to her in her waking hours and Bill encouraged her to write them down. She was very surprised when "This is a course in miracles" flowed from her pen. The information came from a soundless voice which gave her "a kind of rapid, inner dictation" which she took down in a shorthand notebook. She could interrupt the dictation whenever she chose. Whenever she took up her writing again, it would continue wherever she left off. The following day she would read her notes to Bill and he typed as she dictated. The Course evolved over seven years, and today it is printed just as Bill originally wrote it down. Almost no editing was required except for the deletion of a few personal references and the addition of chapter headings and subheadings. Anyone who has done much writing will have an appreciation for this, it being a miracle in itself.

Eventually three books evolved, the three making up the complete Course: a 622-page Text; a 478-page Workbook for Students, with 365 lessons; a Manual for Teachers, in question and answer form. The Course curriculum is very complete and offers both theory and practical guidance. It emphasizes "application rather than theory" and "experience rather than theology." Although Christian in statement, the Course deals with universal spiritual themes. (The material is available in book form from: the Foundation for Inner Peace, Glen Ellen, California.) It emphasizes that it is but one version of the universal curriculum. Most important for me was the statement that "a universal theology is impossible but a universal experience is necessary." I have always trusted experience and so I was strongly influenced by that statement.

Some of the ideas are startling and difficult to accept at first. Helen states in the introduction, "you need not believe the ideas, you need not accept them, and you need not even welcome them. Some of them you will actively resist. None of this will matter or decrease their efficacy." She adds, "But do not allow yourself to make exceptions in applying the ideas the workbook contains [giving over control], and whatever your reactions to the ideas may be, use them. Nothing more than this is required."

Study Requirements

The Course requires a commitment of time and study, but combined with the 12-Step programs it is transformative and powerful. Most 12-Step groups offer tremendous support, providing emotionally non-addictive relationships as we exit from destructive ones or move into recovery from an emotional breakdown, substance abuse, or any other unhealthy addiction.

Healing, in both 12-Step programs and A Course In Miracles, involves a gradual process, slow and continuous. We begin with our false beliefs and proceed at our own speed. Recognition that we are addicts and that we require a powerful, meaningful, belief-changing program, reflects our awareness of the depth and force of our illusions. Understanding this, I believe, is the beginning of wisdom.

Reprogramming ourselves and changing our addictive or illusory beliefs is the work of a lifetime. I am frequently grateful for the trials in my life which have focused me on these solutions. I was not a believer in medication, even after more than twenty years as a psychiatrist, until my own breakdown showed me their live-saving value. I taught others to feel feelings and reparent themselves for nearly fifteen years before I was forced to take my own medicine and go within and deal with my own emotional dependency and discover and then heal my inner child. The first miracles I recognized in my life began when I let go, joined Al-Anon adopted the principles of the 12-Step programs, and began to change my beliefs.

I am convinced that combining the elements of this program offers the opportunity for not only recovering but for transforming our lives.

Meditation—Path to Inner Peace

In reflecting on my years of saying Hail Marys, and more recently the spiritual slogans, readings, and daily reflections related to the 12-Steps and A Course In Miracles, I realized that I was practicing the first stages of an activity known for centuries but seldom associated with psychotherapy—meditation. It is the beginning stage for retraining our thoughts and beliefs, moving from a fearful, self-centered view of our lives to a trusting, God-centered, spiritual view.

Meditation is the core of most spiritual programs. There are steps to the meditation process just as there are steps to 12-Step programs and learning how to "feel our feelings." I have already discussed the steps for process, reparenting ourselves emotionally, and the 12-Steps for treating unhealthy addictions. What follows are the steps for the meditation process.

Steps to Meditation

Although I did not realize it at the time, my first experience with meditation began with my fingering my black rosary beads as a child—kneeling on our living room floor after supper with my mother and brothers, restlessly counting the minutes when at last the "Our Fathers" and "Hail Marys" were done. My mind wandered constantly. I could never focus on the "mysteries of Jesus' life" as we were supposed to do. Too many of my own mysteries were swirling in my mind to concentrate on Jesus. I concluded from that experience, and later attempts to learn spiritually oriented visualization, that I was simply not a meditator.

I had not realized that in meditation, as in life, it is impossible to be an expert on the first try. No doubt there are spiritually advanced Catholics who can meditate deeply and reverently on the mysteries as they say their rosaries. And no doubt there are runners who can complete marathons and yogis who can bend their bodies almost to a closed jackknife position. But they are not rookies. They had to begin at the beginning. It is the same with learning to meditate.

Before even beginning the actual practice of meditation, it can be useful just to have a basic understanding of what we're trying to achieve. Put as simply as possible, meditation is "focused awareness." When we meditate we seek to be in the present moment. I believe slogans and mantras repeated over and over are forms of meditation. They are used to shut out painful or self-defeating thoughts that arise in the immediate present. What I have been calling Process for nearly twenty years—remaining in the present moment with feelings and not running from them—is one form of meditation—a constant, present awareness of our emotional selves.

When we actually do the 12-Steps in healing, they are a form of meditation, too. There are several ways this is true. First, we accept the surrender steps (Steps 1–3) where we give over control of our thinking and beliefs to a "power greater than ourselves." Next we work the action steps (Steps 4–9) to clean up the "wreckage of our past," whether the damage we did was to ourselves (which is very often the case), other people, or both. Each day we continue to stay current in our relationships with others (Step 10). The first phase prepares us for the others. Surrendering control prepares us to "clean up" our past life and helps us to "make the past be the past" so that we can begin living in the present. The second phase, helps us remain in the present by correcting mistakes and resolving issues with ourselves and others on a daily basis. Finally the last steps focus us directly on meditation and its partner, which we know as "service to others."

In meditation, once we are able to tolerate the present—accept the thoughts and feelings we are having—and are able to clear up past issues, we can focus our awareness on our thoughts, feelings, physical sensations, and even our distractions. We give all these inner experiences permission to exist—just as they are. This is the final stage of meditation. It leads us gradually within as we accept and love whatever we experience unconditionally. As we master these steps this gradually becomes a way of life.

Focusing and remaining in the present moment can lead us to our healing addiction—the addiction we began seeking at birth yet only found as we learned to remove the barriers we built up in childhood. As we do this we reconnect with our inner divinity, and live in the present moment more and more consistently and continually.

Going Forward

Through our spiritual reprogramming, we begin to relate to truths greater than ourselves, and to begin drawing strength, support, love, and security from other people and other sources outside us. There is an interesting contradiction which occurs at this point—that the more we become aware of our identity in terms of a source greater than ourselves, the more we come to appreciate our individual responsibility to ourselves and others. The unfolding of this realization is what I call "individuation," the subject of the next chapter.

INDIVIDUATION—
ANTIDOTE FOR ALONENESS

Individuation means taking responsibility for ourselves.
We cannot surrender autonomy until we have attained it.

–THE AUTHOR

Simply put, individuation means "being ourselves." It involves an ongoing, lifelong process toward being less dependent on anything which is outside ourselves. The concept refers mostly to emotional independence and is measured by our ability to be happy and content within ourselves primarily, without needing others—and this includes other substances and other behaviors—to reassure us or bolster us emotionally. It is our strongest antidote for the toxin of unhealthy addictions, particularly the compulsion to please others. However, a more clearly defined self strengthens us against all unhealthy addictions. As a result we become less likely to give over total control to drugs and alcohol, behaviors, other people, or to our beliefs about ourselves, all of which are the hallmarks of unhealthy addiction. We maintain self-control instead.

Becoming an individual is not part of our genetic makeup; it is a learned skill, since all of us begin life being totally dependent. The skills of individuation help us build our emotional strength just as physical exercise develops our muscles. The strengths we gain through individuation skills help us break free from the enslavement of our addictions. We accomplish this by experiencing and becoming desensitized to our fears rather than yielding to them.

We begin the individuation process by paying attention to our feelings and sitting with them in a way that is conscious and aware, rather than acting on them. We learn to be quiet rather than speaking out, or to wait for several hours, or even days, before responding to our hurts. This is not the same as "stuffing" our feelings, when we numb ourselves to our experiences. The difference is that, as an individuation skill, we attune ourselves to what we're feeling. We are not making the decision to "do nothing"; instead, we are making the decision to get to know ourselves a little better by becoming increasingly familiar with the contents of our feelings.

While sitting with our feelings and getting to know them is an important part of the process, there are also times when individuation means taking risks and expressing ourselves. There is no fixed pattern because individuation is the process of learning to take care of ourselves rather than depending on someone else. This process begins with taking care of our own feelings.

We can, of course, err in the direction of too much self-dependence. Once again, becoming balanced is the key. Being individuated should not be confused with "rugged individualism" and the myth that no one else can be trusted. It means that we can choose in our relationships, and that we are able to distinguish between wanting someone and needing them.

Our levels of strength and individuation are constantly in flux. Sometimes we feel confident and are much more individuated than at other times when our confidence is wavering. As we become more individuated we move away from unhealthy addictions and toward healthier ones, all the while learning the meaning of becoming more dependent on ourselves.

As we become more individuated, for example, we may become temporarily "hooked" on ourselves and our autonomy, which makes us seem self-centered. Behavior of this kind can be an important step in the direction of liberating ourselves and feeling the power of our autonomy. This self-dependency is frequently an important phase on the pathway to healing.

Individuation begins when we look inside ourselves for answers, when we stop blaming others for our feelings and begin relating to our emotions and intuitions as our teachers. As we learn to do this more and more, we begin to feel secure and independent enough to risk letting go of everything outside; we begin to trust ourselves instead. This skill is learned through a step-by-step process of asking ourselves for opinions and answers instead of asking other people; it is learned by experiencing discomfort or fear and waiting for answers instead of tranquilizing or numbing our feelings.

Steps in Becoming Individuated

There are three main steps in the process of individuating:

1. Bonding. Becoming emotionally close. Bonding most often refers to an intimate human relationship and is a basic need in all of us. The ability to bond is the first step in healthy individuation. Bonding appears to have a biological connection, and studies have shown that animals who fail to bond, also fail to reproduce and seldom survive. Although we bond, connect, and relate to others in many complex ways and for many reasons, we primarily bond for survival and comfort. People who are able to form stable "bonds" in their relationships traditionally do better and generally live longer and healthier lives than people who do not bond well and live alone.

2. Separation. This means distancing ourselves from someone to whom we are bonded. In infancy, for example, if there is a healthy bond between the infant and parent, voluntary separation is a sign that the infant feels safe and is ready to reach out into the world beyond the mother. In each later stage of life (childhood, adolescence, and adulthood), we undergo this same evolution.

Healthy separation follows healthy bonding. For instance if we do not have comfortable bonding experiences at any stage of our emotional development, it can become difficult for us to trust others or ourselves enough to separate gradually from them and thus grow emotionally. Instead we try to bond in a dependent way in all our relationships, choosing mates, friends, and even business associates with whom we share a mutual fear—the fear that we cannot survive without them. The failure in this individuation process is the basis for virtually every unhealthy addiction.

3. Individuation. This means becoming ourselves and having feelings, opinions, and beliefs that are independent from the people with whom we have bonded. Successful individuation implies that we have been able to bond, then separate, and then learn to operate in an independent emotional mode. After we have bonded with someone and then separated from them, we are able to have our own identity. Let's look at an example from infancy that becomes a model for all individuation processes that follow.

Individuation Model

Early in life, the infant and mother bond, then gradually separate, and the infant individuates as an infant. The infant then reaches beyond the mother, becoming interested in other people, toys, objects, nature, etc., and begins individuation. When the bonding is secure between mother and child, the child and the mother both take pride in their own individuation and the individuation of the other. In the ideal situation, both parent and child have the sense of more deeply appreciating and loving both themselves and the other person. Under these circumstances, the child continues to separate and individuate with ease. In each stage, from infancy to the last moments of adult life, these three steps continue to recur and operate in every relationship of our lives.

Childhood is a time for beginning school, choosing one's own friends, and exploring life away from the protection and influence of our immediate families. If there has been secure bonding, then the separation and individuation occur easily and naturally at this time. If not, the child may feel ambivalent, and even avoid establishing new contacts.

Adolescence is a time to try out social roles, to imitate peers, and to rebel against the established order, whatever it may be. This is when most of us put the final touches on our adult personalities.

For most of us individuation does not proceed as easily or smoothly as I describe above. We become addicted rather than individuated, which then requires that we seek out some outside forms of help. Many times a solid marriage or deep friendship can provide the healing atmosphere we need to complete our individuation process. Or a combination of psychotherapy and healing will allow us to learn these steps. I believe that for most of us there are endless opportunities to grow and individuate, forming new, healthy bonds, separating, coming back together to renew the bond, more fully realizing our own individuation each time. Our awareness of the steps I describe allows us to make use of the opportunities that life offers us to complete this process, rather than moving decisively sideways and repeating the same addictive patterns that have previously ruled our lives.

In any new relationship—or in any relationship that is changing—we bond with the new person at our present level of individuation. For example, we tend to be unconsciously attracted to people whose needs are similar to our own—though they may appear quite different on the surface. Many times we wear masks which disguise our dependency and another person may be attracted to this mask personality rather than to the real self beneath the mask. The reason for this is that we all harbor at least a slight hope that we can find that wonderful someone who will meet our addictive needs permanently, making it unnecessary for us to ever have to individuate. Because of this we all tend to find the spouse, as well as other relationships, which mirror where we ourselves are on the journey toward individuation.

Characteristics of Individuated People

Let's look at some of the characteristics we develop as we become more emotionally independent and individuated.

1. Appropriate emotional boundaries. Individuated people can set emotional limits on how much or how little they allow other people or outside influences to affect them. Healthy boundaries are a protection against unnecessary hurts, and they develop gradually as we change our beliefs and become skilled at deciding where our own responsibility begins and ends in our relationships.

I distinguish between emotional boundaries and the emotional walls that many of us put up in childhood, walls that are called

190 • *Magnificent Addiction*

defenses. These are shields that protect us from being hurt but go far beyond that, also preventing us from interacting with other people or developing ourselves more fully. These defensive postures isolate us behind walls built of fear, whereas our individuated boundaries are formed by choice, allowing us to be flexible, capable of moving or changing the boundaries whenever we wish.

Walls lock us inside, while boundaries operate more as windows, allowing us a choice of what to let in and what to ignore. For example, the fully individuated person might have very definite boundaries defining physical contact with strangers but that same person is able to enjoy deep physical intimacy with a loved one whom they know is trustworthy. Having appropriate boundaries implies that we are able to say Yes and No when we want to, and that we trust ourselves in our choices and consider ourselves okay. We don't constantly ask "What's wrong with me?" when we encounter people with whom we don't agree. When we make mistakes we are able to view our errors as something to be corrected, not a tragedy, and not evidence of our own shortcomings.

When our boundaries are clear we become much more steadfast about our own feelings and our motives for doing things. Defensive and fearful behavior become less and less a part of our life experience.

2. Ability to be alone. Individuation means taking responsibility for ourselves. This often begins with taking responsibility for keeping ourselves company—becoming our own best friend. We learn that being alone does not mean that we have nobody with us. I am all I have and that's enough for me for now," might be seen as the motto of the individuated person during those times when he or she chooses to spend time alone.

As we connect to our feelings and intuitions and discover our spiritual selves this aphorism increasingly makes more sense.

3. Ability to surrender control. Once we have a self, once we have begun to discover our individuation, we become secure enough to give up control. But it is not until we have acquired the autonomy of the individuated person that our fears can dissolve enough to relinquish this control. As we individuate we stop the process of transferring our unhealthy dependencies to others, and we learn to search within ourselves for answers. We give in and surrender, not to other people, but to our feelings and intuitions. Becoming individuated gives us the courage and strength to trust ourselves and leads us to continue our search for healing within rather than outside.

4. Ability to give up judging others and begin forgiving them. When we look within ourselves for answers we can give up always comparing ourselves to others and constantly competing with them. We can relinquish our judgments because our energies are directed somewhere else, becoming fully ourselves. Eventually we discover that comparisons to others are irrelevant and we learn that we already have everything we need. In this way we can forgive others because we realize that despite what they did or didn't do, we have all that we need to heal—within ourselves.

What Individuation Is Not

1. Being isolated. Many people confuse what we are calling individuation with isolation. In deciding if we are isolating ourselves rather than individuating, it is important to look at our motives for that decision. If we feel more comfortable being alone because we are shy and embarrassed around other people, or because we give others the power to make us feel good or bad according to how we believe they see us, then this is isolation, not individuation. In a way, one of the goals of individuation can be the ability to enjoy being alone, that is, enjoying our own company. While this is true, individuation also means that we are at ease being alone, not withdrawing because of our fears.

2. Total control. When we are individuated we feel more in control, not totally in control of our lives. Prior to individuation, control is often manifest as a belief that we cannot feel secure unless the external environment, including the people in it, are in total compliance, or near total compliance, with how we think things should be or how we believe people should act. The un-individuated person often feels that it is dangerous to give up control; in that state, cooperation usually means having other people do what we think they should do without our having to tell them. Negotiating, bargaining, compromising, and surrendering can all seem like sheer madness because they all imply the possibility that we're not going to have everything our way. Individuation is a comfortable state where we want relationships but don't require them.

3. Total self-sufficiency. Total self-sufficiency might be equated with the stereotype of Western culture which we have labeled "rugged individualism," a belief that only our own individual needs matter, and those needs come before anything else. It is the belief that we are "sufficient unto ourselves." If given a voice, the totally self-sufficient person might say, "I have never experienced bonding with another person, don't intend to, and don't need it."

While we become more self-sufficient as we individuate, we do not reject the importance of bonding as an important and essential part of the human experience. We are able to let go and recognize our "interdependence"—with other people and the environment, and this allows us to acknowledge a higher self or God.

Individuation is not the entire answer but it is an essential step on the pathway to healing.

The Joys of Growing Up

Individuation is simply growing up. As grownups we first look to ourselves for help or answers, and our growth may be measured in part by how much we turn to other people or institutions to fulfill essential needs in our lives. We may no longer require psychiatrists, churches, or 12-Step groups as we individuate, yet we may choose to remain connected with them in a new and less needy or dependent way.

As we individuate we are able to change our relationships with 12-Step groups and give more to others. We may find ourselves taking more responsibility in our psychotherapy, in spiritual decisions, and in all our relationships. We can begin to give to others because as we individuate and learn to search within ourselves we discover that we already have everything we need. We give out of a sense of our own abundance then, not because we feel that helping or giving to others is the only way we can prove that we are of any worth.

Efforts to explain individuation often seem to be filled with contradictions. Yet, during those moments in our lives when we experience it fully there is no sense of contradiction, conflict, ambivalence, or doubt. On the contrary, the experience is one of personal fulfillment, of peak experience. Even terms such as bliss and ecstasy have been applied in searching for adequate descriptions. While many reasons might be offered for why individuation helps to supplant addictive behavior, the simplest, most direct explanation is one offered by a patient of mine. "It just makes me feel a lot better than any fix I've ever had!"

Moving Forward

While individuation is a requirement for healing, it is important to emphasize that it does not mean we are "sufficient unto ourselves," or that if we want anything in life we're going to have to grit our teeth, take control and tough it out, trusting nobody and nothing but our own ability to exert control over our environment and other people. As often as not it means knowing when and how to ask for help, establishing relationships which help us increase our strengths. To alter an old saying slightly, "We individuate when we learn how to fish rather than asking others to give us fish."

As we individuate, it is easy to swing the pendulum too far in the direction of control. To better understand this, set us go on to the next chapter, Surrender—Antidote for Control.

SURRENDER— ANTIDOTE FOR CONTROL

We surrender in that most desperate moment of our lives— drawn, pushed, or catapulted into a state of surrender, into our- selves, and now are forced to choose whether to remain there or return to madness.

The idea of surrender can be repugnant to the addictive mind. The very word calls up images of "giving up," suffering, defeat, loss, and even victimization. It is a word for the weak and ineffectual, for people who are powerless or who fail to achieve in life. It is clearly an "un-American" concept! Yet, if as I believe the addictive need to be in control is the source of our pain, then its opposite, surrender, is the solution.

Surrender Is a Choice

Surrender is a decision, a choice we make, one that begins the moment we recognize and accept that we are no longer in control—of either our lives or our emotions. Surrender comes by acknowledging that we are powerless, though we had always been taught to believe that we must be in charge at every turn. This desperate moment can take place when we become too weak, too afraid, too confused, or too out of control to resist facing the truth any longer. Then we finally surrender. We accept that our lifelong belief that control would bring us all we wanted is an illusion; we cannot sustain it any longer.

This event can be dramatic, as it was for me, but that is not always the case. I have known many people who have sunk slowly into depression, not realizing that they were no longer in control of their lives and emotions. I have seen others gradually deteriorate from abusing drugs or struggling through addictive relationships, before they finally reached this conclusion. And there are many others who live for many years with only a vague sense of unhappiness; they eventually choose to surrender simply because they have tried everything else. Still others resign from life halfway through the journey, settling into a fixed set of beliefs. They endure chronic illnesses or unhappy relationships and stoically wait for their illnesses, or simply old age and death to release them from their prison.

All too many people seek help from physicians or other helpers, taking medications to alleviate their pain, yet never look within themselves for their solutions. This is submission, not surrender. Although it may seem like a contradictory statement, this passive victim role is just another way of maintaining an illusion of control. These people live their lives as if every new disaster which they invite into their lives is only further evidence that they are "right." From this they derive their illusion of control.

Many people are skillful in the language of surrender yet they never give up control. Some do this by becoming involved in lengthy psychotherapy, for example. Others do it by becoming deeply affiliated with a church, temple, or synagogue. Still others do it by attending 12-Step recovery groups and becoming very knowledgeable in the concepts of the program. They learn to comply with the prescription for surrender yet often still hold on to the illusion and the need to remain in control. Their compliance to the system, whatever it might be, gives the illusion of surrender but it is actually one more way of holding on. When we play at the edge of surrender this way, we are like addicts who hold back some drugs after pledging to give them up. This "reserve supply," hidden just in case they need it, is referred to as a "stash," and it is anything but surrender.

For years I held on to my stash, though in my case the stash was control, not drugs. I played a role, learning the language of surrender first in psychotherapy and later in 12-Step recovery groups, always living on the edge, forever holding on to my stash and never completely letting go of control. My control was wrested from me by my breakdown. Then surrender seemed my only choice.

There are many programs available—est, Lifespring, and The Summit, to name a few—that teach the opposite lessons, that tell us we can control our lives and that this is our ultimate goal. They reinforce the illusions of our need to control. Many of us explore these and other similar ideas, examining every possibility, and exhausting every kind of relationship until we crumble under the power of our own hurt. This forces us to say, "I give up. I cannot control my pain."

When we bottom out from drugs or suffer an emotional breakdown we experience the loss of control in its most fearful form, but there are also great positive insights that we gain. Everything but our pain suddenly becomes irrelevant. Affirmations of our worth bounce off our skin like minuscule rain drops. Images of success, pride in material possessions, financial security, prideful recognition, fantastic sex, anything which gave us comfort before seems meaningless and unsatisfying. Even if we believe in God we find no comfort. We seem to have been abandoned as we are haunted by relentless depression, the threat of recurring panic, or constant anxiety and dread. All our efforts to find consistent relief suddenly seem futile. It is at this point that we begin to consider other alternatives, because now we must. We have no other choice. Our past seems like a barren, meaningless shell, filled with emptiness, and nothing we own or have accomplished in our lives provides anything more than a temporary and meaningless "fix." It all barely makes a dent in our fears and despair. We retain—hopefully—only enough energy to survive.

I arrived at this place on November 1, 1981, when my defenses collapsed in a heap as I opened the morning mail. I surrendered when I seemed to have no other choice. It was painful and dramatic but I capitulated at that moment. I no longer had any illusions about being in control. I knew I was not. It took many months of medication, more than a year and a half away from work, and 12-Step recovery meetings too numerous to count, before I was able to resume my life. My surrender seemed sudden and dramatic, but it wasn't.

Invitations to Surrender

A year before my apparent breakdown, shortly after my wife and I had purchased the small house we planned to convert into a psychiatric clinic, our request for rezoning the land on which we planned to build had been turned down by the local planning commission. I could have stopped then and sought other alternatives, but I refused. I faced many other hurdles: resistance from neighbors, difficulty finding financing, and the beginning of an economic recession. All of these were messages to let go of that project. Only now do I recognize that each one of these was an invitation to surrender. I resisted. Instead of surrendering I plunged ahead. I ignored friends who advised me to abandon the project. I even suppressed my own fears. I stubbornly chose to listen only to my ego.

I am now convinced that even this last series of events was just a continuation of a long stream of events with similar themes. It was time to examine what I had been doing in my life. Two divorces, many changes in life style, moving my practice from place to place, and continually trying new therapy methods, were all symptoms of my attempts to maintain my illusion of control. If the failed attempt to construct a building had not triggered my breakdown, I believe some other impossible challenge would have.

I was learning that the incidents that occur in our lives are merely symptoms. It is not the drama or the events in our lives that are important; it is their underlying, sometimes hidden messages. We draw to ourselves incidents and relationships that will bring us face to face with our deepest fears. Because my greatest fear is financial disaster I am convinced that I would have continued to take financial risks until I collapsed from some other, similar series of events.

Surrender Is Not Supported By Our Culture

Our culture teaches us that we must maintain control. It does everything but encourage us to learn about surrender. Most advertising is directed not at our spiritual growth but at making us more— better, brighter, thinner, prettier, younger looking, more fun-loving, more handsome. Our culture encourages us to acquire things that will win us the approval of others or gain us recognition as a unique or special person, so that we can feel admired and cared about, if not loved. Our culture teaches us to hold on to the illusion of control by reaching outside ourselves for new cars, new cosmetics, new fitness programs, new "spending power," new soaps, new foods, insurance plans, that will bring us respect, love, security. Everything which massages our egos—lulling us to search for external pleasures instead of showing us the way to inner joy, directing us to search for acclaim rather than peace, or sensory satisfaction instead of sereni-ty—contributes to our addiction to control and our fear of surrender.

Surrender Involves Total Trust

Why is surrender so difficult? Surrender is like pregnancy; it is all or none, and we cannot be a "little surrendered" any more than one can be a "little pregnant." Surrender involves totally letting go of control. And surrender requires total trust. If we have any reserva-tions, if we hold back even a tiny bit, or if we are merely beginning to trust, this is not surrender; it is still control. Surrender tolerates no compromise, no halfway measures.

The total trust involved in surrendering is not easy. It helps us understand why we hold on to our stash so tenaciously. Addiction involves the opposite of trust, which is control. When we are addict-ed to anything it allows us to maintain the illusion that we are in control. An alcoholic, for example, believes he can choose when to drink, and how much; he sustains this illusion of control with "I can stop any time I want to." Relationship addicts, so-called "people pleasers," believe they do it for love, never acknowledging that they are not in control of their addiction. This example can be extended to emotional disorders as well. Emotional breakdowns, depression, panic attacks or crippling obsessions, as well as many physical disor-ders, result from trying to deny and control feelings that cannot be controlled. Healing, I learned from my own experience, can only take place when we are totally free from fear, even temporarily, and only when we are able to trust totally can we achieve this.

But who do we trust? Who can we trust totally? This is the dilem-ma of the addict who has bottomed out and whose life is in chaos. It is the predicament of those of us with emotional breakdowns who fear the return of our painful symptoms and know that our solutions are beyond our domain. Most of us have previously chosen to trust only ourselves and have empowered and deified our addictions. When we break down or bottom out we learn that we cannot be both the source of our problems and the solution. If we could trust ourselves, if we could remove our own fears and obsessions, if we could lift ourselves from depression, if we really were in control of our addictions we would not crash, or break down.

Surrender is ultimately a spiritual issue, not a psychological one. We can only totally surrender to a power greater than ourselves, and usually we call that power God. Only God is qualified to be trusted totally and thus our only safe surrender is to God.

All of us have experienced what happens when we naively trust someone who seemed trustworthy, only to be hurt, disappointed, or disillusioned. *The San Jose Mercury News* recently uncovered a confidence scheme which cost many sports celebrities from the San Francisco area a total of several million dollars. I can relate their calamity to my own when I invested in a limited partnership several years ago, after vowing I would never do so. I made an exception and entrusted my money to the promises of a suave, silver-haired land developer, and I watched helplessly as my investment quickly disappeared. Even the best human relationships are not perfect; even when they seem to satisfy all our human needs, they are guaranteed to end when we die. Nothing in our world satisfies the requirements for total trust. Ultimately we discover that God is our only remaining option, and our best one.

Total surrender which results from total trust does not happen quickly for most people. I have read of miracles and have observed miraculous transformations in my patients over several years, but surrender and trust require steps. Though surrender must be total, we only trust, we only let go one instant at a time. Short of having a miracle happen, our most dependable route to surrender can be found in the following steps.

Steps to Surrender

Step One: Medication can be helpful as a first step for those of us who feel out of control from emotional breakdowns or who have used alcohol or other self-administered drugs for relief of symptoms. I have described how important medication was for me during the early months of my recovery. When we have disrupted the chemistry of our brains, and distorted our biological rhythms, the skillful use of medications can help us regain enough inner control to make choices, and we regain an ability to choose to surrender. The subtlety of this is not apparent to many physicians who staff chemical dependency units and who condemn the use of any drugs in the treatment of alcoholics and substance abusers. Surrender requires total trust, and medication can often serve as a bridge, a temporary symbol of a trusting relationship, an indication of the physician's support in beginning the healing process.

Step Two. Learning to trust our feelings, our intuitions, our inner sense of what is right or wrong for us is another step in the surrender/trust process. As we saw in the discussion of individuation, we can learn to reparent ourselves by recognizing and accepting our feelings, by becoming desensitized to our buried pain, and by processing our emotions rather than acting upon them.

Step Three. Finally we look beyond ourselves, to a power greater than ourselves, to whom we can surrender control. Someone who is totally trustworthy, totally dependable, totally loving, totally powerful, someone named with words such as "God," "Higher Power," "Allah," "Creative Life Source," or others. It does not matter whether we locate this power or presence in ourselves or in the heavens, whether we use the name of Nature, Jehovah, Christ, Mohammed, or Buddha, and whether we affiliate with a religious group or have only our own relationship with this Energy. What matters is that we are able to trust without reservations and are finally able to surrender control.

People who suffer from panic attacks are particularly fearful of trusting anyone, yet they offer a clear example of how developing total trust can transform their lives. Unfortunately they are caught in the dilemma of not trusting themselves either. I have always felt a special compassion for these patients because their quandary seems so obvious yet so painful to observe. I have seen how their trusting me and my recommendations—for using medication, learning to trust themselves and their feelings, even the scary and painful ones, and ultimately their spiritual surrender as they learn to totally trust the God of their understanding—has transformed their lives.

One of my patients, a psychiatric nurse, was crippled by her panic attacks five years ago. She could not go into restaurants for fear she would have to use the bathroom and would have an "accident." She feared giving up any control; even taking medication made her feel panicky and guilty. Yet medication helped and she gradually was able to trust enough to take sufficient dosage to eliminate her panic attacks. She struggled for two years learning to allow herself to experience her fear and to recall buried events from her childhood. And finally, when her son nearly died from an overdose of drugs and was hospitalized in a chemical dependency unit, she entered the program as his "significant relationship" and found a God she could trust in the 12-Step program. It was then that she began to feel a peacefulness she had never known. And gradually she was able to lower the dosage of her medication without a return of her fears.

Surrender-like Experiences

I believe the urge to surrender is always in us, always competing with our need to feel in control. Surrender is often simulated in life, often attempted by trying to have the experience of giving up control on our own terms. This is what leads to unhealthy addictions, the struggle for relationships that we believe we can control. This struggle hides behind many masks, remains disguised behind secret fantasies and desires which are never fully satisfied. We want to let go. We want to depend and feel accepted, loved, admired, nurtured, respected. Even the most self-sufficient of us harbors a longing to be cared for—no matter how deep our life's experiences have buried that fantasy, and no matter how fearful we are of trusting others. We want to maintain our control of the letting go. We seek to control what we would relinquish. How do we do this? Where do we look? There are many examples:

Drugs. Letting go can accompany the experience of "having a few drinks," or the use of recreational drugs. Relaxation, freedom from worry, and the loss of self-consciousness all simulate the peace of mind we are seeking. Only the present moment, the "now" exists when we're "under the influence." There's only you and me. Drugs can provide all these feelings. They can dissolve fear and I believe they can help us to transcend our everyday reality, allowing us to exist only in the moment. In the short run, they allow us to experience something very close to the feelings that true surrender brings.

My patients who have taken LSD or other mind-altering drugs, and those who have taken MDMA (popularly known as Ecstasy or "Love Drug") describe such experiences. Some believe their experiences with these drugs uncover or reinforce their belief in God. Drugs have an appeal as a painless shortcut to peace of mind and instant spirituality. Often they are used in some religious rituals in this way. Peyote, an LSD-type drug, is used in some Native American religious practices to induce a transcendent experience, in which the participants are released from the ego's constant demands for control.

Falling in Love. Falling in love is another surrender-like experience. When we fall in love we temporarily collapse our ego boundaries, relinquishing our defenses. We feel as if we have transcended our limits. We feel powerful, confident, at peace, and tranquil; we feel free of fear, insecurity, and self-doubts. It is a wonderful experience—one of life's best—while it lasts. But this is not surrender, any more than drug experiences are, because it depends on someone other than ourselves. To have this form of surrender we must go from person to person, dependent on the excitement of the body and the senses. Complete surrender teaches a different kind of lesson; that we are joined in spirit but our bodies can never merge except through illusions and fantasies.

Wheeling and Dealing. Entrepreneurs and other "wheeler-dealers" often describe the heady feelings of high finance in surrender-like terms. Fear and caution are dissolved by a sense of power, much as with drugs and falling in love. Again, the source of this surrender is "out there" and it depends on something other than ourselves for its generation. Power is a drug. And the feeling of transcending the boundaries of ordinary living fuels much of our society.

Sexual Orgasm. Orgasm involves letting go of control, too, and is perhaps one of our most familiar surrender-like experiences. In an intimate setting lovers experience the "illusion of fusion." They feel a sense of oneness, union, and transcendence of their individual boundaries; they seem to merge and unite briefly, retaining a glowing memory that lasts for minutes or longer. We seek to experience that feeling again and again. Yet its lack of perfect satisfaction leads eventually to sexual boredom or a continued search for transcendence with other partners. The release of energy in sexual orgasm requires a release of control impossible for many whose addiction to control is trapped inside their bodies, making even this degree of relinquishment or surrender too fearful. Women who cannot achieve orgasm and men who cannot ejaculate hold back from fear, often convinced they will "lose themselves" in this experience.

Nature. Some people find a sense of surrender in the majesty of nature, the beauty of multicolored mountains, the raging power of the ocean, the breathtaking infinity of the sky on a star-filled night. They feel merged with the universe, at one with all of creation. The power of the physical world overwhelms our defenses. Control is dissolved—temporarily. For much of my life, this was the closest I ever came to the feelings that surrender makes possible.

I was often lonely in high school. Shy, skinny, and sensitive, my restlessness was buried beneath layers of teenage self-consciousness, hidden beneath masks and a well-learned role of extrovert and entertainer. I participated in sports, had friends, excelled in class, yet I was seldom content. I compared myself constantly to others. I feared rejection. Yet I seemed so normal. I recall my solitary times more than my triumphs—nights when I would feel painfully alone, afraid to reach out and ask for attention, too frightened and ashamed of my needs to risk asking for their satisfaction. There were nights when I would walk alone on the dimly lighted grounds of the Kalamazoo State Mental Hospital, peering into windows, imagining the lives of the patients and how they compared with mine. I fantasized greatness and triumphs that would soothe my pain, praying to the God of my childhood, saying rosaries hoping for relief, yet always hurting because of my presumed imperfections, my skinny limbs, or the surging passion that craved more intimacy than my God would allow. I needed more touching, more recognition, and more reassurance than I dared to admit.

One night, early in the summer, I was walking home from a track competition. I had just won the mile run, my best time well under five minutes. Yet, after I showered and dressed I felt terribly alone and began to walk the three-mile distance home. Walking past the hospital grounds my attention was drawn to a cloudless and star-filled Michigan sky. I recall feeling even more alone, wishing I had a friend with whom I could share this moment. Suddenly I felt as if I were being lifted from my body and becoming part of the night, part of this seemingly limitless scene. I felt that I had merged with the universe. I lost any awareness of my self. My constant self-consciousness disappeared and I experienced feelings I could only feel but never describe. I thought, "How inadequate words are!" I felt what years later I learned was a transcendental experience.

This experience offered me the most surrender-like feelings I was to know until my recovery many years later. In all my years of searching nothing I found out there was as powerful or impactful on me as that summer night. Yet that experience faded as I sought many times, on many other nights, to reproduce those feelings.

All the experiences I describe are surrender-like; they resemble surrender, they confuse us, and we continue to ask, "Why me?" Similarly, resignation to life is not surrender, but a bargain we forge, secretly hoping to win our God's favor. Compliance or any of the roles we learn to play and practice. Humility, sacrifice, or devotional rituals, though they can simulate surrender. They do not meet the unconditional requirements that surrender demands. For me it took so many years, from childhood to my fifties, to fully grasp what it was I was seeking. What I thought was success was only an interim, a precursor to the time when I would relinquish control. I have seen others surrender without a lot of drama, without breakdowns or life-threatening illnesses. Others, I am convinced, find the same answers I have by travelling other paths. No matter. I am convinced that surrender is the one universal experience we all need to go through to be whole.

206 • *Magnificent Addiction*

The Process of Surrender

We are able to grow in surrender much as we grow in understanding, patience, compassion, or any other virtue. We can grow in surrender just as we grow in business, as a friend, as a parent, or in any other way. We grow by practice, by doing, getting a little better at it each time. It is a process rather than an event. Surrender is a decision which must be reinforced again and again until it becomes a habit. By accepting example-by-example, and step-by-step, that people, feelings, and events are out of our control, we learn to surrender. We surrender control, then take it back, thousands of times before we "let go and let God" (one of the slogans of the 12-Step programs). We practice. Surrender. Control. Surrender. Control. Surrender. Control. And gradually we achieve surrender and the cycle changes. Peace. Control. Surrender. Peace. Eventually we achieve surrender and peace.

And finally, peace.

Many of us surrender control to drugs, love, sex, power, and a host of other idols for years before we undertake the final steps toward surrendering control. Recovery programs which focus on trusting God (no matter how that God is defined) substitute an infinite God for the gods of our addictions.

We all seek to transcend the reality we experience when we limit ourselves to the perceptions of the physical body. I believe this is the major attraction of drugs and other ego-dissolving experiences.

Stages of Surrender

Stage One. The Search Outside Ourselves. This first stage is often the longest lasting. It begins with the search outside ourselves. It is exhausting to think about the years and the places I searched. But no doubt I am not unlike many of you who struggle to see how unique and special you are. Our search is always based on the belief that "something out there can satisfy me." Only years of emotional honeymoons, where we feel an initial excitement followed by disillusionment, disappointment, and often depression, over and over again, lead us to question our choices. It is often a major disappointment or apparent tragedy that ends our outer search.

Stage Two. Breakdown. This stage begins when we accept that our lives, or at least some aspect of our lives, are out of our control. Our pain forces us to focus our attention within ourselves; as long as it persists we continue to seek our answers there.

Stage Three. The Inner Search. Most of us avoid this stage until we reach a point of no return, usually as the result of experiencing complete emotional or physical devastation. For many it begins with a lost job, a life-threatening illness, a failed relationship, or even an earthquake or other natural disaster. The single most important part of this step is we look for answers within our own thoughts and feelings.

I want to assure readers that we can learn the lesson of surrender without a total collapse, such as I and many others suffer each year in this country. Each of us has our own agenda, our own invitation in the form of a situation that will give us the opportunity to surrender. Complete breakdowns seem to occur only for those of us who refuse to surrender control until they are rendered powerless by events occurring outside us, or by our own emotional pain. The following story, where breakdown and recovery occurred without missing one day's work, is a much more typical scenario.

Fred, a physician, had been separated from his wife for nearly a year when I met him. Gwen had wakened him from a sound sleep one Sunday to announce she no longer loved him, and after eleven years of marriage she wanted a divorce. She had seldom complained about anything during their marriage. Her only complaints were her frequent physical symptoms, and Fred had never considered those an expression of her unhappiness. Gwen declared he had been "controlling" throughout their years together and she wanted out of their relationship. Fred was flabbergasted. Her first verbal complaint was a proclamation that their marriage had ended.

At first Fred tried for instant reforms. He undertook a crash course in therapy and recovery, hoping to salvage his relationship with Gwen. He acknowledged his controlling behavior but had always assumed Gwen's silence had meant agreement. Obviously he had misread her intentions. He saw a counselor through the Employee Assistance program at work, quit drinking at the counselor's recommendation, and joined Alcoholics Anonymous hoping to improve himself enough to save the marriage. He and Gwen dated occasionally after they separated, usually at Fred's initiation, but after a year they were no closer.

Gwen kept her attorney on retainer and kept Fred on the hook by occasionally kissing him passionately but rarely accepting his invitations to make love. These occasional passionate moments were enough to fuel Fred's hope for reconciliation and Gwen changed her mind about proceeding with the divorce several times. Fred altered his diet, his habits (quit smoking and began a rigorous exercise program), but never changed his mind about wanting to win back Gwen's affection. He continued paying all her bills, filed her insurance claims, cared for her car and funded her spending (Gwen had not worked since they were married) while he lived like a monk. The only outside activities he allowed himself were addressing Gwen's needs and attending 12-Step meetings four or five nights a week.

One night he announced to his 12-Step support group that he had "surrendered." He had given up this unilateral courtship. No longer would he pursue Gwen. No more phone calls. The next move was hers. He admitted the first of the 12-Steps, that he was "powerless over Gwen." He felt elated and peaceful.

Three days later he crashed. It began with insomnia. He thrashed about nightly feeling helpless, unlovable and convinced he would be alone for the remainder of his life. Work distracted him during the day but nights and weekends became torture. He had never felt so much pain.

I encouraged Fred to sit as long as he could with his feelings without reading, listening to music, or having any other distractions. I prescribed a mild antianxiety medication for his disturbed sleep and encouraged him to *do nothing*. As he followed these instructions, he gradually became aware of his inner restlessness and recognized how addicted he was to Gwen. Fred experienced withdrawal symptoms of loneliness, worthlessness, and grief as he allowed himself to sober up, that is, abstain from Gwen, his addiction. He was in too much pain to even consider another relationship. Fred continued my prescription to feel his feelings and allowed himself to surrender to his pain. He hurt so much that he had little choice.

Fred surrendered to his outer world when he let go of trying to change Gwen's mind about the divorce. For the first time he stopped looking outside himself for answers. He went inside—to his feelings—seeking answers. Previously Fred had taken all his cues for his feelings from other people, and he had always performed according to his very skillful reading of their expectations; he felt happy or unhappy according to their assessment of his performance. When he surrendered and began to search for answers within himself he found the source of his fears. Until he redirected his search by giving up trying to rekindle Gwen's love he had not surrendered.

No pain. No gain. When Fred surrendered his efforts to control his relationship with Gwen he did not anticipate pain. He was like most of us. He surrendered only when he had to—when there was no other choice. No one, as I have said—not even masochists—seek pain. We surrender when facing pain is our only acceptable alternative.

Drugs, falling in love, sex, power, and nature are mentioned mainly as preliminaries to surrender and spirituality. They are not advocated as answers—not even temporarily. Most of us have our share of addictions before we surrender. Thomas Aquinas wisely reminded us "there is some truth in every error." Even drugs? Yes, even drugs. Drugs provide a preview of many of the elements of surrender and thus spirituality. Just as with any other error we might make along the way, drug experiences can be part of the search. Each experience is more than an attempt to avoid pain. Many an alcoholic has learned the pain of losing control, and finally surrendering, through the pain of addiction.

Saint Augustine, feasted thoroughly on life before he surrendered and pursued spirituality. As John Donne said, great sinners have become great saints. And wild, crazy searcher/addicts can become loving spiritual role models.

My own path as you see, was far from straight—though drugs were not my addiction of choice. My recovery is less than complete yet I pursue a spiritual course because it's the closest to heaven I have ever come.

If, indeed, it is always darkest before the dawn, perhaps the rampant abuse of drugs today is the forerunner of a new spiritual dawning. Let us hope so.

Staying Surrendered Can Be as Difficult as Getting There

Staying surrendered, not resuming control of our lives, can be difficult. Constancy and steadiness, daily surrender, giving up control and not taking it back—these can be most difficult. The exercises given at the end of this chapter can teach us the concept of surrender, and even acquaint us with what surrender feels like. But living our lives, surrendering to our inner wisdom or to God, is the ultimate challenge and the ultimate reward. We must work daily on the hard kernel of defiance which makes up the tiny amount of residual fear and distrust that we hold on to rather than maintaining a state of constant surrender.

The hard kernel of defiance, wanting to live life our own way, continues to persist. We slip back again and again into doing it our own way. I often tell patients who ask "How long will this go on?" that if the pain is brief, so is our memory of pain. We quickly resume living as if we are in control. Our old companions pride and arrogance are more than willing to spend time with us.

Compliance Is Not Surrender

Many who begin recovery programs approach them like school or career preparation. I did. I attacked the 12-Steps, feeling prideful as I put each one behind me—one by one. There was a brief honeymoon, similar to the honeymoon of a dieter, or any newly separated man or woman who hopes that changing the relationship will solve the problems. During this brief time, I praised the program and basked in the glow of my own pride. Then one day that glow faded and I felt much like I had when I began recovery. The honeymoon was over. Recovery, which requires surrender, is not like school or work. Success is not based on performance. You don't receive a report card or a diploma at the end of the year.

Like Fred and others who are focused on outside evaluations, I complied, worked the steps conscientiously, and expected results. While I complied I did not surrender. Eventually I discovered that compliance is in our head while surrender takes place in the heart.

Compliance is partial and conditional. Surrender is complete and unconditional. Compliance is temporary. Surrender is long term. With compliance there is tension, holding on, resistance. Surrender requires acceptance, relaxation, and peace.

It is possible to work the steps, to fill endless pages in workbooks, keep count of meetings attended, preach recovery to everyone, yet fail to surrender. It is even possible to use recovery programs to defy recovery. We can be modern day Pharisees who keep the form of the 12-Step programs but violate the spirit. It is possible to speak at meetings with eloquence, develop vast libraries of books like this one, read the literature, fill our homes, offices, and car bumpers with slogans hailing the wonder of recovery, yet through all of it cling to control. We can continue to hold on to our hard kernel of defiance indefinitely, as Barbara does in the following story.

Barbara consulted me about her panic attacks. She was becoming more and more fearful, restricting her activities. Her fear of these attacks interfered with her family life. She made excuses for not going out, even though she felt her kids were becoming more self-reliant and did not need her. She hated lying to them and her husband, however, when she made excuses to hide her fear.

She could tolerate almost no medication. But she had little difficulty accepting the idea that she was addicted to her need to look good to others and be in control at all times. She joined our 12-Step group enthusiastically. I seldom saw her for appointments after that but she reported much improvement. On her rare visits her meditation books were thoroughly underlined and obviously used. We both believed she was recovering.

She called one morning to report a "horrible panic attack." She had become furious with God, she related. How could God do this after all her work?

Barbara realized what she had done almost immediately. She laughed and said, "Now I know the difference between compliance and surrender." It was then that she really began to let go of trying to control her recovery.

Surrender Is Not Easy

Raylene frequently spoke of her feelings of shyness in new groups. Like an alcoholic who only needs one or two drinks to feel secure, she could dissolve her shyness if accompanied by one or two friends. Alone, without her "fix," she was always painfully uncomfortable in any new situation.

After therapy she learned the source of her fears and did better. Joining and participating in emotional "encounter groups" helped too. She felt a confident glow after each one of these highly charged experiences. Yet, the results were never apparent when she was around strangers again.

When she joined a Codependents Anonymous group, she worked the steps diligently. Yet her shyness persisted and she became discouraged. Her therapist, a veteran of "compliance without surrender" helped her to see how she was trying to control her recovery by "working" the steps and "expecting" results.

She began to understand recovery. She surrendered control in group situations, did not attempt any roles, or techniques. She learned to let go of trying to control what others thought of her in these situations. She said the Serenity Prayer over and over each day. She learned to surrender and accept God's will rather than her own.

Raylene is healing at last. Still, one cannot help but wonder if that hard kernel is still operating inside her. However, I know that as her therapist I need to surrender control, too. I am powerless over the outcome of my patients' struggles to surrender.

We Do Almost Anything to Avoid Surrendering Control

Surrender is not for everyone. It is a commitment. It requires weeks, months, and years of preparation for most of us. We have to try everything, again and again and again, before we even consider it an option. People can use psychotherapy and 12-Step recovery groups to avoid change and avoid surrendering control, giving the impression of change yet never changing. We learn the language of surrender, holding on to that hard kernel of defiance and self-will all along. We surrender only when we have to.

Being in a position of authority or power can help us avoid surrendering. Politicians. Judges. Attorneys. Teachers. Physicians. Psychiatrists. Clergymen. The list could go on forever. All have a hundred ways of saying "I'm okay—you're not." Needing to feel in control may motivate choosing these professions. No matter what our job or profession we all choose control over surrender.

What do we surrender? We surrender control of feelings, substances, other people, life circumstances, fears, obsessions, depression, panic—the list could be endless. Until we surrender we cling to the illusion that our salvation lies in learning to control these, and more. Eventually we learn that it is an illusion that never rewards us.

Surrender Is an Option; It Is Not a Requirement

Some people continue to choose suffering and the illusion of control over surrender. That sad scenario is only too familiar. We humans have an endless list of ways to deceive ourselves in this regard. We can resist surrendering control by neglecting our health, by remaining in destructive relationships, by deceiving ourselves with fantasies about our talents, life goals, or other people.

Every life offers constant invitations to surrender. Any crisis is an invitation, and if we continue to attempt to exert control in the face of it, crises will demand our surrender, forcing us to change, if not for the better, then for the worst. The answer always sounds like such a contradiction—to let go of trying to change the unchangeable and surrender to the reality of the present.

These invitations have names. They are called burnout, breakdown, bottoming out, disaster, catastrophe, bankruptcy, divorce, abandonment, cancer, heart attack, or stroke. You may think of others but these cover most of the situations I see.

We are like Humpty Dumpty. When we break we don't have all the king's horses or all the king's men available to put us back together again. Our healing begins by accepting the invitation to surrender, to place our trust in a power greater than ourselves.

Crisis can take endless forms. Perhaps a family member dies. Or we have an accident. Or our spouse asks for a divorce. Or a relationship fails. Or we are arrested. Or we have a whole series of crises. Or we simply grow older and one day realize that we must surrender to our mortality. We read the obituaries and see contemporaries checking out. Eventually we all have such crises—and we break. Only God, with our consent, can put us together again.

We can refuse to give our consent. We can continue to live life the way we choose. Surrender is always an option. It is not a requirement. For some it comes just before death. A few die unyielding and in denial.

My brother Bob was a wonderful man. A loyal son and brother, and a devoted priest for more than fifteen years. Later, when he resigned from the priesthood and came to California, he worked as a counselor to students at the University of California at San Diego. He served in this role for more than ten years. He was determined to retire at age fifty, which he did. He worked very hard with that single goal all those ten years. He had become disillusioned with religion during his years as a priest because of the bureaucracy and pettiness of the Church. He was determined. He was stubborn and proud. Two years after his retirement, he was diagnosed with terminal lung cancer.

This was not in his plan. He endured pain without complaint. He was loving to his last breath. He finally surrendered but not until shortly before he died, too many years before his time. It was from living helplessly through this experience that I began to learn the lesson that he learned so late.

The Principles of Surrender Simplified

The spiritual principle of surrender has become a keystone of our lives. We have discovered that when we surrender, God will do for us what we cannot do for ourselves. But what are the dynamics of this principle? What actually happens?

The first thing that must occur is for us to reach bottom—to become sick and tired of whatever it is that has been making us sick and tired: a character defect, an old idea, an unhealthy relationship, an obsession, or an illness—relatively minor problems as well as serious ones.

Following that, we must accept our powerlessness, conceding that it is futile to keep fighting the person, place, or thing causing us difficulty. We must also concede that it is beyond our capacity to fix the situation. We admit that we need help from a power greater than ourselves.

What usually happens at this point is that the negative feelings that have festered within us—anger, resentment, fear, and above all frustration—become greatly diminished. Because we have stopped trying to do things our way and have begun to approach the situation calmly, it becomes possible for God to enter our life and bring about change.

Clearly, the act of surrender relieves us of the burden of our addiction to the illusion of control. We acknowledge that our addictions were ineffective, returning us again and again to that which we most feared. In the process of reparenting ourselves, we learned that what we had feared—our own feelings—did not need to be avoided or controlled. This is the point at which we begin to discover our spiritual identity, a source of strength that far surpasses any form of control we might be able to invent. We discover that our real source of love, peace, and security is not achieved through our personalities or egos but was there all along. It was merely hidden from us for the moment. This spirituality is the subject of the final chapter of this book.

SPIRITUALITY—
THE ADDICTION THAT HEALS

*Until my own emotional breakdown I failed to address
the possibility that my perception of being abandoned by
God was an addiction, a fearful compulsion to be a god to
myself, to deify beliefs, substances, other people, and behaviors
which left no room for discovering the God of love. We will
always be addicts yet it is the addictive commitment
to God and our spirituality that ultimately heals us.*

Spirituality is one of the many ways we define our life experience. True spirituality is also an addiction—though in this case it's a positive one. It is surrendering control of our lives, not to fear, as we do with unhealthy addictions, but to a power greater than our own egos.

Spirituality, like other addictions, is a consuming, all-or-nothing experience, not unlike the mind set in unhealthy addictions except that the outcome is different; when we are spiritual we feel profoundly different than we do when we are addicted to a drug or a codependent relationship. Instead of momentary relief or brief pleasure followed by pain, we perceive a sense of peace and contentment. Instead of seeking to control relationships, as we do with our unhealthy addictions, we experience a sense of safety which dissolves our fears and allows us to surrender control with the assurance that we are safe and secure in doing so.

Just as there is no such thing as being "a little pregnant," there is no such thing as being "a little spiritual." And we are never "just beginning to be spiritual." When we surrender to the spiritual it is total or it is nothing at all. The periods of time that we remain in this state of surrender may vary, but within each of those periods—no matter what the duration—our surrender is total. In each moment of surrender we experience a deep sense of conviction and security about our lives, which one of my patients clearly defined when he remarked, "I don't believe in God during those times when I am letting go and in touch with my spirituality. At those times, I know God."

An Energy Discovered through Feelings

We first discover spirituality as an energy which guides and empowers us; it provides the inspiration for an artist's painting or a writer's poem, or manifests as an urge to look upon strangers with love, or inspires us to have unusual courage or take risks. Spirituality is most easily recognized at its intuitive, feeling level—as the feeling of Oneness with the universe that we get when we gaze into the apparent infinity of the heavens in a star-filled sky, or the sense of peacefulness and joining that comes to us when we observe an infant delicately cradled in its mother's tender embrace. Experiences like these give us a sense that we are connected with something or someone very powerful, an entity which replaces fear with awe and wonder.

We say the above experiences are spiritual because they touch a place within us that is beyond the scope of our ordinary senses, impossible to measure scientifically. But even these pale in comparison to what it is possible for us to feel in the state of complete surrender to our spiritual essence. Spirituality of this kind reaches deep into our very beings, filling us with a perception of profound safety, removing all pain, soothing all our senses, at the same time allowing us to feel total and complete as individuals. At such moments we have no perception of fear, not even when disaster seems to be pressing down on us in the external world; our existence seems to be totally in the moment. As we look out we feel fused and connected with everyone else as well as with the whole universe.

For many of the people I have met in my work as a psychiatrist, the fleeting spiritual experiences they have are rarely powerful enough in themselves to set them on a committed spiritual pathway. Only deep and long lasting inner pain seems to have the power to do that—the power to create an emergency so impelling that we begin seeking this ultimate addiction and looking for ways to systematically maintain it in our lives.

The Addictive God of Fear

Many who reach the point of spiritual emergency unfortunately become quite confused about which way to turn. Their confusion is based on childhood experiences associated with old religious teachings, for example, the portrayal of God as vindictive and punishing. These people often find it so difficult to acknowledge God that they even turn away from 12-Step groups. They are psychiatrists and other physicians and professional helpers who consider religion to be the opiate of the masses, and these are the people for whom the word "spirituality" holds negative meanings, painfully associated with old and unpleasant experiences concerning God's demands.

In childhood we may have learned a wide range of rote responses memorized in catechism classes, or subjected to countless theological explanations and innumerable interpretations and misinterpretations of the Bible. For so many people there is the fear, stemming from childhood religious teachings, that makes it difficult to trust God, or even to believe for a moment that a higher power exists.

It is difficult to develop deep trust in our spiritual identity when the prevailing attitudes about God in our culture are so unloving. The addiction to fear and to a wrathful God, a God of fear, makes it impossible to find a God of love. How do me make the transition from the God of fear to the God of love which we can trust totally? Only the Eastern religions seem to have accomplished this; their beliefs reflect a God who is more consistent with the experiences of peace and oneness that we have discussed here. But what can we do short of studying Buddhism, or a related religion, if we wish to gain this kind of spiritual insight?

Fortunately, we can learn the process of giving over control to the wisdom of our intuition and feelings; as we do this we begin to heal, learning to reparent ourselves by giving ourselves permission to experience and nurture our own emotions. We discover that we truly do have our own inner teacher, one that reaches beyond our pain. Our inner guidance speaks to us through these instincts and feelings, ultimately helping us arrive at a personal definition and experience of spirituality. As my patient observed, when we follow the pathway of our inner teacher we do more than discover God. We know God.

Barriers to Spirituality

Unhealthy addictions have awesome power, blocking our discovery of our true spiritual nature. By constantly surrendering to the false authority of our unhealthy addictions, and our ever present need to feel that we ourselves must be in control at all times, we can delay too long. We can end up with the kind of bodily deterioration that physical illnesses can bring, or we may suffer the crushing torment of emotional breakdowns. Our unhealthy addictions stand in the way of our most potent antidote for fear—that antidote being love.

It is important to recognize that fear is the hallmark of all unhealthy addictions, addictions which block us from looking within or listening to our intuition and feelings. It is fear that keeps us from finding inner spiritual wisdom—the kind of discernment and insight which are our healing source.

As we have seen, only pain seems to have sufficient power to melt the barriers that we build up throughout our lifetimes. These barriers are the products of our egos, which rally their most potent weapons in an attempt to defend us from fear. Most of us open up and rediscover our spirituality only when these weapons of the ego fail us—and they always do, no matter how our egos deliver the blows intended to block our fears.

Spirituality and Religion Are Not the Same

For many of us the word "spiritual" rekindles painful associations with church and religion that we may have learned in childhood. This was certainly true for me, even though I have some happy memories about my early religious experiences as well.

So many people associate spiritual and religious terms with a punishing or angry God from our pasts. It is impossible to separate the "father" or "mother" God from experiences with our own parents or parent surrogates. God can be associated with parents who controlled us, or worse, who abused and rejected us. How do we believe or trust in a God who might be like our parents? Many of us simply can't. Spirituality for us is too often associated with painful memories of a bearded fellow with a massive head and angry face warningly pointing towards hell. These images are many times too painful and vivid to allow us to connect the words *love* and *God.*

In more traditional homes we may have learned to envision the religious brand of spirituality as a commodity which we are able to purchase with good deeds and personal sacrifices, or even through a set of rituals and practices that would secure God's support. My early religious training as a Catholic convinced me that my efforts were capable of earning double bonus points in heaven, called indulgences, which would reduce my sentence in purgatory after I died. My failures would doom me to an eternity of punishment. This is great training for fear and for addictive behavior; but it is hardly good preparation for loving spirituality.

In spiritual programs which teach love in the place of fear, and where there are no threats of punishment, there is no need for a great ledger in the sky where our good and evil deeds are sorted and recorded. A God of love neither judges nor condemns us. The unconditional love that we discover within ourselves, as a result of following the healing program described in this book, truly mirrors God's love.

If there is a God who bargains and keeps score in heaven, then the ego's ultimate wish seems to be fulfilled—proving that man or man's ego can control God after all. The absurdity of this notion is perpetuated because our culture and many traditional churches have adopted such a God, a superior being who operates on the basis of rewards and punishment, success and failure, winners and losers. Only a society that measures us by our performance could devise such a God, a deity who allows only men to be ordained, who ostracizes gays and lesbians, who sends Catholics to different places than Protestants after death, and who neglects anyone else. This wrathful, unforgiving, score-keeping God has become part of our problem, not our answer.

Memories that many of my patients associate with God can range from the boredom of endless hours spent in church to beatings and sexual abuse inflicted by parents or even religious teachers who spoke of God. Such memories make those who have been on the receiving end of such abuse fiercely determined never to risk surrendering their hard won adult independence and control to anybody's God.

One can easily see how negative memories associated with God and organized religion can make the road to spirituality a difficult one. How can we trust anyone outside ourselves after a childhood of being controlled, abused, or abandoned? How can we surrender control when it is associated only with fear and pain? We must first melt our defensive barriers, ones that seemed, and perhaps were, so necessary in childhood. Time and patience are necessary to locate the God within. Let me share an example with you.

Mickey was raised by two parents he adored. Unfortunately they both were alcoholics. When either of them drank their personalities changed. Mickey's dad, a police captain, became critical and belittling. From a man Mickey idolized he heard constant criticism and reproach. He recalled painful times of being called "fat ass" and slapped for no apparent reason in front of his friends. Once Mickey's father made a pass at Mickey's high school prom date. As the result of all his father's abuse Mickey had turned into an adult who was tremendously self-conscious and hypersensitive to criticism.

Mickey's mother became embarrassingly promiscuous. Mickey was witness to a stream of nameless lovers wandering in and out her bedroom. He became filled with shame and embarrassment. He felt abandoned by them both. And he learned to bury tons of rage.

When I met him he was a trim, muscular twenty-five-year-old fireman, trained as a paramedic. He was fair skinned with blond hair cut in marine style and blue eyes that made our unmarried receptionist fidget. When he smiled he looked like a guileless little boy in a man's body. Except for bold tatoos on both arms he could easily have passed for a male model. Yet he was still self-conscious and felt like the "fat ass" his dad called him, pointing out a tiny donut of fat around his abdomen which few would ever have noticed.

He was ten months sober from alcohol and prescription pills. It was his third time around in recovery. He was depressed, besieged with obsessions, and desperately seeking anything that might help quiet his pain. And he trusted no one. He began to have faint feelings of trust in me since many of my symptoms prior to my healing were similar to his own. He tried acupuncture, gestalt therapy, hypnosis, vitamins, astrology, and faith healing during the time he was consulting me. He could find no solace in 12-Step meetings. Spirituality was just a word. I continued to offer him support in trusting his feelings and waited patiently month after month for him to melt the walls he had built to survive the painful abandonment of the alcoholic parents he loved and needed so much. At one point he became addicted to four- and five-hour daily workouts and I didn't see him for more than six months.

When he returned his obsessions had lessened and he had begun to experience his pain—his hurt and his rage. His cherubic smile was gone now, replaced by eyes that often overflowed with tears. His boyish features tightened and the muscles on either side of his jaw seemed to be constantly taut. Mickey raged for weeks. He cried, shouted, cursed, and fought to control his impulses to commit mayhem—or worse. Somehow I never worried that he would. He seemed to have a core of caring, integrity, and self-control that told me his perception of his parents was probably accurate. They had loved him deeply whenever they could—before alcohol consumed their spirits.

Mickey began to heal. After he exhausted his pain he began gradually to connect to his love and gentleness, which I always knew his smile reflected. His face softened and his boyish good looks returned as he was able to relax and recapture his engaging smile. He connected to that loving child within, which was still alive and well beneath the abandonment, hurt, sadness, and rage. He connected to God—through his own inner being. He was at last able to begin trusting again and finding meaning, solace, and comfort in the spirituality of his 12-Step recovery.

Mickey's story is a dramatic example of the importance of connecting first with our inner selves, the often bruised, crying, abandoned child within, before we can unite with our spiritual selves. Until Mickey connected with that child and his pain, his search for spirituality was mostly in his head. He trusted only his thoughts, constantly obsessing over his futile efforts to feel in control and not surrender. The patient, frightening journey to connect with that child was achieved as Mickey allowed himself to experience the buried fear behind his painful obsessions. Uncovering his hidden feelings of rage, fear, and abandonment ultimately led him to the still-healthy child within. Through this process he also found the God within. I'll never forget the day he first made this connection. He just stretched out his long legs, hugged himself, and smiled.

He was still sitting there, alone, content, and at peace when I left the room to attend a meeting with my staff.

Spiritual experiences such as Mickey's take place inside our hearts, within ourselves—within the divine, loving inner child that lives in each of us. Mickey clearly discovered this and has since gone on to trust his relationships with that child within. Now he feels safer in having close relationships—even with his mom and dad. Last summer he took his fiancée—no, it was not our gorgeous, unmarried office manager—to meet his mom and dad who are now both in Alcoholics Anonymous programs of their own.

What Is Healing?

Healing is the process which reconnects us with our saving addiction, that is, our spirituality. The process involves far more than simply relieving symptoms. It consists of a combination of methods which address our problems at every level. I searched more than twenty years before I discovered that my knowledge and understanding of spiritual principles was flawed. Until my own emotional breakdown I failed to address that my perception of being abandoned by God was an addiction, a fearful compulsion to be a god to myself, to deify beliefs, substances, other people and behaviors which left no room for discovering the God of love. We may always be addicts, yet it is the addictive commitment to God and our spirituality that ultimately heals us.

Although there are many other spiritual programs with the same goals, I believe that 12-Step programs offer distinct advantages for large numbers of people who cannot afford expensive psychotherapy. They also offer a belief in spirituality which is rare among psychotherapists. And most importantly these programs emphasize the importance of surrendering control to God as a condition for healing.

How to Do All the Right Things and Still Be Unhealed

The same people who have left traditional religions can remain unchanged and unhealed in 12-Step programs or in any other spiritual program. This is not to make light of their efforts by any means; I am simply saying that there is no simple formula for becoming spiritual. The way to become spiritual is to involve ourselves in a process whereby we upgrade our addictions until we become addicted to love. It requires an emotional commitment, one which is total and never ceasing, a commitment which begins with a momentary surrender and extends in time until the moments grow into minutes, hours, and days.

True spirituality is an addiction—total, unrelenting, and unconditional just as God is. The three essential steps that help us begin giving up self-centeredness, willfulness, and pride are simply stated. They involve: 1) Surrender, 2) Detachment, and 3) Acceptance. These steps launch a frontal attack on our egos. These are the efforts by which we "till our inner soil," helping us create a proper physical, emotional, and Godly frame of mind, allowing us to experience what spirituality really is.

Healing then is not a reward for hard work, perfect church attendance, sacrifice, meditation, good family background, genetic engineering, or anything else. Healing is our birthright, given when we remove the barriers we have built up and invite it into our lives— when we admit that we are powerless to help ourselves and ask. The

God of love pursues us gently, often for years, before we open the doors and show even the least interest.

The Gift of Grace

The name for this gift of healing comes from the Latin root *gratis* which implies that it is freely given. It is a gift offered by God. He does for us what we cannot do for ourselves. Dr. Gerald May, in his book *Addiction and Grace*, points out that this gift is recognized in all major religions. It is the energy, the power, the miracle which heals our destructive addictions and redirects our energy into the addiction of love.

In 12-Step recovery programs we find this expressed in the phrase "We do the footwork, and God controls the outcome." Grace allows us to move beyond the limits of our human limitations, beyond our illusions, beyond our need to be in control, beyond the skill of psychotherapists, physicians, and other healers. Grace rewards our faith and trust—the spiritual "tilling of our inner soil." It is the gift we receive when we surrender to the God of our understanding.

One of my mother's favorite sayings was "Live as if everything depends on you. Pray as if everything depends on God." Not bad advice.

God offers us choices. God offers not just the choice to recover from our addictions, as we have seen, but something much more: He offers the choice of the only addiction which will satisfy us—the addiction to love, which only his gift of grace makes possible.

A Return to Spirituality

I reluctantly resigned from the Catholic church during the 1960s. It was particularly painful for me to separate from a church with so many wonderful traditions, including the excellent Jesuit universities such as Marquette, in Milwaukee, where I received my undergraduate and medical education. It was painful to leave a tradition that had long been a part of my family life—two of my brothers were priests—and which was connected with my best friends from childhood and college.

Following my separation from the church, I remained busily unconcerned about spirit or spirituality for nearly twenty years. I frantically searched for answers everywhere else, as I described earlier, trying to fill the huge void that leaving Catholicism left in my life. Like many of my patients I confused spirituality and religion. The baby went out with the bath water. When I walked out of church I forgot about God. In truth I was angry at God. I felt let down and betrayed. I associated God with Catholicism. And I thought the Catholic church owned God. During those years, and even today, I find myself uttering "Hail Mary full of grace" or reciting other prayers I learned in childhood, during times of stress.

I told myself I had left the church because it no longer helped me in my adult search for answers. Celibate, unmarried clergy making eternity-binding policies about marriage and birth control made no sense to me as I struggled with marriage and five young children who were born from passion. To survive as a family we could not rely solely on "Papal Roulette," as we called the rhythm method, which was the only form of birth control acceptable to Catholicism in that era.

I left the church in angry frustration as I daily confronted the inequities I had to deal with every day in my work as a young psychiatrist. Every day I saw people whose problems could not be solved by the Catechism, some of those problems so great that suicides were not uncommon. The organized religion I knew seemed unable to respond realistically to the human problems of the day. As a human system, it was all head, with no heart. The solutions it offered seemed to be compassionless, never considering the emotions with which all of us must struggle as human beings. If there were a God it seemed silly that he could have created feelings but had only approved one or two of them—mainly guilt and fear. That God seemed to busy himself as the great scorekeeper in the sky—keeping track of trivia.

The more I connected with my own emotions and learned ways of dealing with them, the less interest I had in the church. In encounter groups, personal relationships, and in the gatherings of others seeking to find answers at Esalen Institute in Big Sur, California, I discovered feelings I had never experienced, or perhaps had repressed so many years ago that I had forgotten them. I began to experience feelings other than in my head or my penis—the two places where both Catholicism and psychiatry focused most of their attention. Beyond the limits of Catholicism, with its emphasis on morality and theology, and beyond psychiatry, with reverent emphasis on Freudianism and drugs, I began to experience other realities unfolding for me. I discovered differences between sensual and sexual, considered solutions between black and white, beyond the either/or choices of life. And I discovered wonderful, loving feelings in places and under circumstances that my confessor would have condemned. Out there beyond church and religion, past analysis and better living through altering brain chemistry with psychiatric drugs, I found my passion.

I returned to life after years of being a fearful child trying to live by outdated, cold, theological formulas that sucked the life energy from my loins. It was "out there" beyond all that I had been taught to believe that I found love and support and permission to begin looking "in here"—to my feelings—for the answers. That was the beginning. I risked. I made mistakes. I gave up my head for quite a while, but in the process I found love. I found my heart.

I gradually continued to search wherever my heart and feelings guided me. It was not easy. Each time I took a new turn other people in my life were affected. My first wife, Gail, my children, my patients, my friends. Even our family dog Sheba could not adjust to one move and went to live in a more tranquil and unchanging home. These were liberating experiences for me but I know only too well that they were sometimes painful for others in my life. And many of my actions along the way were definitely not spiritual.

The direction of my search changed abruptly after my dad and three brothers died during the 1970s. Dad had been in ill- health for years, but his sudden, painless death in 1972 abruptly confronted me with my own fragile mortality. And then, over the next several years, my three oldest brothers slipped away, one by one, after valiant struggles with cancer.

The pain I felt with each of those losses gradually contributed much to my depression that followed. Each loss forced me further inside myself, further into a life lived mostly trying to win other people's love, admiration, and respect through outstanding performance. I began to understand that the emotional highs which accompanied the first breaths of freedom, as I broke away from the "parents know best" institutions in my life, were really expressions of delayed parturition, cutting the umbilical cord which should have been cut long, long ago. Depression became more and more inescapable as each portion of my security blanket dissolved, my inner darkness becoming my unwelcome but inescapable teacher. The more losses I experienced the more meaningless my prior "searching" seemed to become. Finally D-Day (the Great Depression of Dr. Kavanaugh) occurred in November 1981.

Spirituality, as I now know it, began for me three and a half years later when I connected with 12-Step recovery at an Alanon meeting held in St. Christopher's church in San Jose, California. Ironically, perhaps, it was Mother's Day. I had been away from my psychiatric practice for more than a year, healing from anxiety and depression. I had been off all medication for several months and had recently returned from staying with my brother in southern California. An on-again, off-again relationship with a girlfriend I considered "alcoholic" had suddenly blown up and I was once more depressed and seeking comfort in Alanon—an organization for "the friends and relatives of alcoholics."

There, for the first time, I let go, and publicly admitted I could not solve my problems alone. I surrendered to the God of my understanding. I cried that night, tears of relief and joy mixed together. And I experienced a peacefulness that I had only known for brief moments before. Over and over I continued to repeat a line I remembered from Saint Augustine—the patron Saint of my parochial school in Kalamazoo—"my heart is restless until it rests in Thee." I found comfort in this.

The spirituality I discovered that memorable night requires no theology, no defined concept of God, or good and evil. Collections and tithing are not prescribed. No sin, confession, or fasting. No sacrifice. No knowledge of the Bible is required. No familiarity with Jesus, Buddha, or Confucius. And best of all, no guilt.

After I began healing I recognized that the highs I had experienced in encounter groups and other peak experiences I had during the years of searching were more like "fixes," similar in many ways to a fix from drugs or sex—temporarily satisfying but not lasting.

One by one I examined what I had felt were answers during those years and I realized the source of my good feelings was always from outside me. Each high depended on something or someone "out there." Besides I realized that a part of me had always known that this was true. What is most important, though, is that the best of those experiences paled next to the experiences I am able to have, at times, on my present internal, spiritual journey.

As I learned more and grew spiritually I experienced great joy, which slowly drew me deeper and deeper into myself—into the realm of spirit. I found that from time to time I would come to a place I had maybe never known during nearly forty years as a devout, practicing Catholic.

I learned that this new spirituality has an attractive, almost seductive quality that calms and comforts and heals. And almost effortlessly I have wanted to know more about Jesus, Buddha, Mohammed, all the great saints. Freud and even Jung pale by comparison with these giants. I am fascinated by the simplicity and sameness of each of their messages, and after years of being bored by spiritual reading, and turned off by the myths of psychology and psychiatry, I find myself alive, interested and passionate, seeking time and space to follow this path.

My search only began with an answer I found in 12-Step recovery. I hoped it would end there—with a sudden magical transformation. But the answer I found merely changed me from perceiving myself as a "seeker" to perceiving myself as a "finder." I had searched out there for most of my life, but found my answer only within me. Now, at last, I realize that's exactly what I had been hearing and reading—but never quite fully grasping—for years. I love the expression, "When the pupil is ready, the teacher will appear." It tells the story of our personal journeys as few aphorisms do. Importantly the 12-Steps had provided me with a structure, proven to be successful for so many others who had gone before me. It offered me a path to follow, ultimately taking me to the trailhead for my spiritual journey home.

I often review the search of the past twenty years and ask myself how did I get from there to here? I think about the years of searching and compare it with the contentment and peace I often feel today. The answer, so long in coming, is simple. The process of change began and ended with pain. When I could no longer run or avoid pain, when I was finally forced to follow it inside to its source, and then learn to listen to my feelings, I began to find what I had been searching for.

Pain—when it continues for a long time, as mine did—is a very persuasive teacher. Like so many people I avoided mine as long as I could. Eventually, after holding me hostage for so many months, I was forced to pay attention, surrender, and do as my pain dictated. If I demurred, the pain was back again. My pain "sentence" convinced me that I do not want to try any of my old answers again. That knowledge continues to make my internal journey easier.

I have finally found an addiction—the addiction to love and God—that requires no money, no endless supply of drugs, no sexual encounters, not even a "special" relationship. With this addiction there are no hangovers or regrets, no unpaid debts or lung cancer, and no need to control or please those around me.

Stages of Spirituality

My spiritual path began that painful and memorable night at a 12-Step meeting. It continued when I attempted to halt the pain I discovered there with constant repetition of 12-Step slogans. At first I counteracted my painful and fearful obsessions—which had occupied almost every waking moment—with these slogans. "It's out of my control," and "Let go and let God" were my favorites. I discovered I could temporarily crowd out painful thoughts by constantly repeating these sayings. I began to be reminded of the Hail Mary's from my childhood, or the frequent repetition of litanies and rosaries so familiar to Catholics.

There were times I believed I would wear out the 12-Step slogans because I was repeating them so much. I told my patients, "If you had any idea how many thousands of times I repeat these slogans you would relax and be patient with yourself. It takes a long time to reverse the thoughts and fears of a lifetime."

I continue to employ these slogans as my first line of spiritual growth. For several years I carried them on small 3x5 cards in my shirt pocket. Later I substituted other slogans and sayings on cards from A Course In Miracles and I constantly searched for other spiri-

tual first-aids to use when sudden or unexpected fears overloaded
my still-fragile circuits.

Walking a Spiritual Pathway

I sometimes reflect on the life I have today, and I cannot help but
compare it with the life of my past. I find it difficult to claim any
credit for the changes, nor do I any longer blame myself for taking so
long to begin looking in the right places for my answers. I believe
that we must all look outside ourselves until we have exhausted all
the fantasies and all the possibilities we have constructed from our
less-than-perfect childhoods.

Today I know the God of my understanding lives within me. We
are inseparable. I have more and more moments, and even some
hours, of experiencing the unity of the universe, of seeing us all as
one. I welcome quiet and enjoy being alone more than ever before. I
require less sleep and I believe there is a divine plan, a belief which
often quiets my impatience. After the many years of struggling I
finally recognize surrender and accept that there is a God—one that
is even more powerful than I once thought I was.

Relationships are still important to me but not desperately so as
they were in the past. Nor does criticism cripple me for days or
weeks, as it once did. My world is more inside me. My heart has
moved from my sleeve to inside my chest, where it was when I began
my life. The gnawing fear of economic ruin, my most constant companion since childhood, only creeps inside when I stay "out there" for
too long at a time. When I forget to meditate, when I stop hanging out
with others who are healing, I once again start listening to the insane
rambling of my ego. Its story is always the same, that I can be safe
and secure and peaceful only if I give it complete control of my life.

One learns not to argue with the ego. But I still gently remind it
that none of the things it told me I must fear for so many years are
happening. I also remind myself that I care for myself better yet am
less self-centered; living in the present allows more time to think
about others. I spend more time alone yet am immensely less lonely.
I surrender control frequently yet feel more powerful. Pain is not as
painful and fear is not so frightening. Age is a blessing more than a

curse. And, finally, death only means I no longer have to watch this body deteriorate.

And now, I only occasionally find myself asking, "Why did it take me so long?"

Childhood seems much longer ago. More important, I see it as a time of passage, thought this is something I've been able to see only after I relived the painful past in process and became free to recall and relish the happiness I experienced in those early years. Most of the time I see my childhood only as preparation for today.

My joy from the triumphs of my favorite sports team, or my misery when they lose, fades more quickly.

Winning at tennis, racquetball, or other sports churns my insides more gently and softly—though I grew up with competition in sports as a religion, just below the Church in rank. It's a relief not to be driven by it anymore, able to enjoy sports as a calmer, more satisfying pastime.

I accept my years of struggle, including the years of prolonged depression, my prior addictions to work and to relationships, as well as the long frustrating process of healing, as parts of the teaching each life requires. The pain of those years was clearly fueled by my own efforts, my ambition, my greed, and my constant push for control.

More than anything else I feel gratitude. Gratitude that I am ever more conscious of being my only enemy. Grateful for the parents, brothers, wife, children, patients, and friends I have. Grateful for my experiences, my struggle, and finally my patience in writing all this down. I look upon those who might otherwise be my enemies as my teachers. I have grown to feel content with "progress and not perfection."

I am most grateful to the God of my understanding who invited me repeatedly to listen and surrender, yet waited lovingly and patiently for me to discover what was always true. I found God when I found myself.

The search is over. The journey is unfolding.

SLOGANS FOR DAILY LIVING

The principles of this program are nicely expressed in slogans that can help us cope with symptoms or stress everyday living situations when we repeat them over and over. Repeating these ideas is the first stage in learning to reprogram unhealthy beliefs and replace them with new, fulfilling ones.

We recommend that they be written on 3x5 cards and carried with you for ready reference during difficult times. The slogans represent healthy beliefs as formulated in the Process model of this program, the 12-Step model, or A Course In Miracles.

Slogans for Dealing with Control

The major area of difficulty in living is learning to deal with control. The Serenity Prayer addresses this so well and helps us learn what we do and do not have control of in our lives. It is very helpful to repeat this prayer often, on a daily basis:

God grant me the Serenity
To accept the things I cannot change,
The courage to change the things I can,
And the wisdom to know the difference.

For Worry

Other slogans that are helpful in situations where we feel worried, frustrated, or out of control:

Let Go, Let God.
Turn It Over.
It's Out of My Control.
I Am Exactly Where I Am Supposed to Be.
There Are No Accidents.
There Is a Plan.
Progress, Not Perfection.

For Self-Consciousness

In situations where I am self-conscious or afraid around people, or am upset or bothered in a relationship because of trying to "control" what others think of me or giving others the "power" to make me happy or unhappy:

What others think of me is none of my business.
What I think of me is all that counts.
Just stay true to my feelings.
Stop trying to be someone I'm not.
It is more important to be honest than nice.
No one can make me feel badly unless I give them that power.

For Impulsiveness

For times when I feel impulsive or harried or hurried and feel I'm going out of my mind. For those situations where I am trying to control the uncontrollable:

Easy Does It.
Think Before I Act.
Think.
I Cannot Control Outcomes.
Feel the Feelings. Don't Act on Them.
Turn It Over. Let Go, Let God.

For Frustration and Guilt

For times when people-problems are frustrating, especially in the family or at work. When I feel guilty or responsible for someone's life or behavior:

It's Out of My Control.
I Didn't Cause It. I Can't Control It. I Can't Cure It.
No One Can Make Me Feel Bad Unless I Give Them the Power.

For Self-Doubt

For those times when I have self-doubts and really wonder about myself. When I am confused and don't know what to do or am afraid that I am doing the wrong thing:

Trust My Feelings.
My Feelings Are My Truth.
Make a Decision. Call Whatever I Hit the Target.
I Am Exactly Where I Am Supposed to Be.
God Did Not Create Any Junk.

For Unhappiness

For times when I am miserable and unhappy and tend to blame someone else for my unhappiness:

It Is My Job to Make Me Happy.
No One Can Make Me Feel Bad Unless I Give Them the Power.
Feel the Feelings. Don't Act on Them.
I Am Exactly Where I Am Supposed To Be.
Others Are Okay the Way They Are.
My Unhappiness Is My Responsibility.
Feelings Are Not Caused by Anyone Else.
I Cannot Change Anyone But Me.

For Guilt

For times when I feel guilty about one of my decisions, or when I feel guilty for no good reason or about things over which I have no control (like the past):

Feel the Feelings. Don't Act on Them.
Let Go, Let God.
I'm Exactly Where I'm Supposed to Be.
Progress, Not Perfection.
It's Out of My Control.

Living at the Heart of Creation
by Michael Exeter

Living at the Heart of Creation is not a self-help manual or a "fix-it" book of superficial answers. It is, rather, an intelligent yet simple offering of insight into such challenging areas as the environmental crises, overpopulation, business relationships, and personal well-being. Michael Exeter shows exactly what it means to live at the heart of creation—to live at the place T. S. Eliot called "the still point of the turning world."

This book will be a friend and companion to anyone with the desire to explore what it means to be vibrant and wise in these extraordinary times.

$9.95

Gentle Roads to Survival
by Andre Auw, Ph.D.

Psychologist Andre Auw, a close associate of great 20th-century psychologists Carl Rogers and Virginia Satir, characterizes people who learn to prevail over life's challenges as survivors. While some are born survivors, for most of us, survival is a skill that must be learned. Using dozens of case histories, poems, and allegories, Auw identifies the lessons all survivors know: characteristics that distinguish people who give up hope from those who find the inspiration and encouragement to carry on.

"I loved your ideas. They contain a great deal of wisdom, wisdom gained from experience."   *—Carl Rogers*

$9.95

Your Body Believes Every Word You Say
by Barbara Levine

This is the first book to describe the language of the link between the mind and body. Barbara Levine's fifteen-year battle with a huge brain tumor led her to trace common phrases like "that breaks my heart" and "it's a pain in the butt" back to the underlying beliefs on which they were based and the symptoms they cause. She lists hundreds of common examples of words we use unconsciously every day, and shows how these "seedthoughts" can set us up for illness.

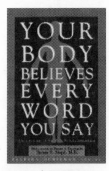

$11.95

Personal Power Cards
by Barbara Gress

A simple, easy to use set of flash cards for emotional wellness. Includes 55 cards, a carrying pouch, and an 80 page booklet. The Cards help retrain your feelings to be positive and healthy. Their combination of colors, shapes, and words allow positive thoughts to penetrate deep into your subconscious, "programming" your emotions for health.

"In the twenty years I have been using color and mind imagery with patients, I have never seen any approach have such a great benefit on self-discipline and self-esteem."

   —Richard Shames, M.D.
  Family Practitioner and author of Healing with Mind Power

$18.95